ALBANIA—

China's Beachhead in Europe

ALBANIA—

China's Beachhead in Europe

HARRY HAMM

Translated by Victor Andersen

FREDERICK A. PRAEGER
Publisher · New York

BOOKS THAT MATTER

Published in the United States of America in 1963
by Frederick A. Praeger, Inc., Publisher
64 University Place, New York 3, N.Y.

© 1962 by Verlag Wissenschaft und Politik, Koeln

© English translation 1963 by Frederick A. Praeger, Inc.

Library of Congress Catalog Card Number: 63–14679

This book is Number 127 in the series of
Praeger Publications in Russian History and World Communism

Printed in the United States of America

Foreword

FOR A LONG TIME it had been difficult, if not impossible, for nationals of Western countries to obtain a visa for entry into Albania. For journalists, such a visa had been out of the question. Since the end of World War II, not a single newspaper correspondent from West Germany had been granted permission to enter the country. The last time any reporter from the free world was allowed entry had been in 1957, and the reports brought back from the most isolated of all Moscow's satellites caused a sensation. Since then, Albania had kept itself rigidly isolated from the outside world. What was happening in the craggy mountainous country on the Adriatic, particularly with the course of political developments, could only be speculated about. Official propaganda handouts and highly doubtful reports and rumors originating in the countries bordering on Albania were the basis of these speculations. The smallest of the chain of Communist people's democracies had turned itself into a kind of Tibet.

It was therefore all the more astonishing that in August, 1961, three of my German colleagues and I received official permission from Tirana not only to enter Albania but to stay in the country for almost four weeks. Western diplomats were certain that the remarkable news was all a mistake which would soon be corrected. Our journalist colleagues made no secret of their envy. Newspapermen from Iron Curtain countries simply did not know what to make of this decision by the Tirana authorities. It was so unexpected and so contrary to all previous practice that newspapermen suspected some political skullduggery behind it. Some of them gave expression to their secret fears by dark warnings about lack of food, the survival of Stalinism, and execution squads.

Uncertainty was also written on the faces of the Albanian officials who received us when our plane landed in Tirana. Their

nervous and over-polite gestures revealed that visitors from the
West, and particularly Western journalists, were as much of a
sensational event for them as our arrival in this forbidden land
was for us. The customs officers tried to give the impression that
their inspection of our baggage was an unavoidable formality.
Even the representatives of "Alb-Tourist," and the quietly dressed
men in civilian clothes who suddenly appeared from nowhere,
seemed to be trying hard to show that they felt the same way.

When we were released from the formalities and went out into
the open, accompanied by smiling functionaries chatting about the
weather, I still had an eerie feeling—an apprehension that is inevitably aroused by the excessive courtesy on the frontiers of a
totalitarian state. But all went well, and we were invited to climb
into Polish-made *Varshava* automobiles for the journey into the
city of Tirana.

After a trip that took us over a first-class road through both
fertile agricultural land and industrial suburbs, the cars drew up
in front of our hotel, the Hotel Dajti, named after the mountain
range that lies beyond Tirana. It was built by Italians, and is the
only hotel in Tirana regarded as suitable for foreign guests. The
courtyard in front of it serves as a platform for the speeches of
ranking Communist functionaries during political celebrations,
and as a plaza from which they can review the parades of the
"toiling masses" marching past.

The enormous structure seemed to be almost completely empty,
and the voices of the yawning staff seemed to echo along the cor-
ridors. As we stood among the large, overstuffed, and unoccupied
armchairs, the atmosphere was that of a morgue. Suddenly a
handful of guests appeared on the staircase. In chattering groups
or one behind the other, they came down the stairs. They were
Chinese.

This was the first real surprise of my stay in Tirana. It was not
to be the last.

Contents

Foreword   ix

I. HISTORICAL BACKGROUND   3

II. FOREBODINGS OF REVOLT   8

III. THE FACTORS BEHIND THE REVOLT   53

IV. ALBANIA AND THE SINO-SOVIET DISPUTE   104

V. ALBANIA AND THE TWENTY-SECOND PARTY CONGRESS   140

Index   171

ALBANIA—

China's Beachhead
in Europe

I

Historical Background

ALBANIA STILL BEARS the traces of its turbulent past, a history that has been the story of a never-ending succession of invasion and defense, of subjection and revolt. At one time or another, Greeks and Romans, Goths and Byzantines, Serbs and Bulgars, Sicilians and Venetians, Normans and Turks have poured into the country and held it for varying periods.

In the first twenty years of the fifteenth century, the Turks conquered the land and took all its towns and fortifications. The Albanian feudal lords accepted their subjection to the power of the Osmanlis, and they became the Sultan's vassals. As proof of their fealty and devotion, they were required to give over their sons to the Sultan for upbringing and military training. It was this custom that determined the career of the greatest Albanian national hero, Georg Kastriota (known in the West under the name of Scanderbeg), at the start of the period of Turkish rule.

Scanderbeg grew up as a Christian, but at an early age he was taken from his parents and removed to the Sultan's court in Constantinople. There he was educated as a Mohammedan and received an excellent military training. In 1441, he decided to return to Kroia, his family home, to make himself an independent prince and to resume the fight against the Turks. From that time until his death in 1468, he carried on an unceasing, heroic fight to prevent the armies of Sultan Murad II from advancing into the heart of Europe. Three times—in 1450, 1466, and 1467—the Turks besieged Scanderbeg's fortress in Kroia, the center of the resistance to the Ottoman advance; and three times they failed to take it.

Resistance to the Turks collapsed with the death of Scanderbeg. Despite his scanty forces, the Albanian national hero had managed to hold off the Sultan's assault for more than a quarter of a century, absorbing the impact of the Turkish invaders and thus

3

playing a decisive role in preventing the overwhelming of West European civilization. Scanderbeg has become the symbol of freedom and independence for all Albanians, a symbol that understandably has a particular attraction today.

The Turks remained in power in Albania for over 500 years, during which their presence gave both the country and its people a new stamp. Many Albanians became Moslems, and many entered the Sultan's service. As *Arnauts,* Albanian soldiers formed the backbone of the Turkish army. Some Albanians achieved positions of high eminence in the Ottoman Empire: a number of grand viziers were of Albanian descent. The Sultan's guard and the Constantinople garrison were selected from Albanian soldiers. The Turks established Albanian military colonies in Greece.

The special position of the Albanians in the Ottoman Empire became an important starting point in the struggle for Albanian independence. South Albanians played an important part in the Greek war of independence at the beginning of the nineteenth century, powerfully supported by the Egyptian viceroy, Mehmet Ali, who was of Albanian descent. In 1878, the Congress of Berlin decided on the transference of certain Albanian border areas to Montenegro. This decision led to the creation of the "Albanian League," which called for armed demonstrations against the ruling of the Congress of Berlin. The "Albanian League" also became the nucleus of a struggle for independence that went on in the decades that followed.

The hour of liberation seemed to have arrived at the end of the nineteenth century, when resistance to Turkish domination flared up all over the Balkans. Montenegro, Serbia, Bulgaria, and Greece succeeded in shaking off the Turkish yoke in the Balkan War of 1912. The Albanians—mistrusting the territorial ambitions of their neighbors—did not take part in the Balkan War, but when Turkish rule in the Balkans crumbled and Constantinople withdrew its troops from Albania, Ismail Kemal took advantage of the opportunity and, supported by Austria-Hungary and Italy, proclaimed the independence of Albania in 1912.

This proclamation of independence, however, did not assure the freedom and independence of the tiny country. There was still the matter of defending Albania's newly won sovereignty against practically all of her neighbor states. The Serbs had already advanced as far as the Adriatic. In 1913, an international statute was agreed upon by the Great Powers to protect Albania's territorial integrity. The Powers appointed a German prince, Prince Wilhelm zu Wied, to rule the country. For six months he did his best to govern the new state, but the outbreak of World War I put an end to his efforts and saw the opening of a new struggle. Serbia had already annexed Kossovo, and now Italy stepped in and took possession of the port of Valona. The Greeks advanced into North Epirus and Montenegro took over North Albania. Albania became a theater of war. Austrian and Bulgarian troops marched into the towns, from which they had to retreat with the advance of French and Italian forces.

In 1919, after the end of World War I, the Treaty of Tirana reaffirmed Albania's independence as a state, and she was accepted into the League of Nations. The borders of Albania were guaranteed by international agreement, but within those borders there was a state of internal chaos. The attempt to introduce Western-style democracy ended in dismal failure. Bitter personal feuds, shootings in the parliament, and confusion in public administration combined to defeat all efforts to bring about conditions of law and order. In 1922, Ahmed Zogu, a member of one of the leading families in the north of the country, elbowed his way through the feuding leaders to make himself dictator.

Zogu managed to keep his position as Prime Minister for a little over a year. The Army brought about his downfall, and he had to flee to Yugoslavia. He was succeeded by Bishop Fan Stylian Noli, whose attempts at reform also failed because of the internal chaos prevailing in Albania. A few months later, in December, 1924, Zogu reappeared in the political arena and once more managed to seize power. With a few thousand Albanians put at his disposal by his brother-in-law, who lived in the border area under Yugoslav control, and a hundred Russians, ex-members of Wrangel's army, he advanced from Yugoslavia. The miserably equipped Fan Noli forces offered only minimal resistance, and Zogu reached Tirana in a few days. Now it was the turn of Bishop Noli and his associates to go into exile. Zogu's revolt was given the high-sounding name of "triumph of legality." The weapons that made his "triumph" possible were provided by Yugoslavia, while the money was furnished by the Anglo-Persian Oil Co., which hoped to find oil in Albania.

Zogu declared himself President of the Republic and lost no time in paying his debts. The Yugoslavs were presented with several "corrections" of the border they thought important, and the British were granted permission to bore for oil. But now Zogu thought it desirable to improve his standing with the Italians. In view of the centuries-old territorial ambitions displayed by Albania's Balkan neighbors, Zogu believed it was important to assure Rome's protection of the young state. He signed a treaty of friendship with Italy in 1926, and in the following year, a treaty of alliance was signed that pledged Italy to a number of military obligations.

On January 1, 1925, Zogu was elected the first President of the Albanian Republic. His constitutional term of office had run only half its course, however, when he had himself crowned King on September 1, 1928. From then on he was known as King Zog I.

Zog was not a democrat. He had no use for political parties and banned them all. Still, he must be given credit for having created a reasonably stable government to replace the chaos and anarchy. His chief failure was in the economic area for the country remained poor and backward. The large-scale land-reform measures which were essential for the improvement of the country's economic conditions were never put into operation, for Zog dared not alienate the great landowners, without whose support his own position might have been imperiled. Zog's achievement in welding the various tribes and family groups into one nation is indisputable, but in the end all his efforts foundered on the social antagonisms and economic difficulties that increased from year to year.

In the foreign-policy field, Zog had begun by setting a course enabling him to tack between Italy and Yugoslavia, trying to exploit the struggle for power between them for the benefit of his country and himself. But as time went on, he began to side more and more with the Italians, who furnished ever-increasing assistance in the way of subsidies and investment. Albania finally became, from the political point of view, an Italian protectorate.

The political, military, financial, and economic dependence on Italy reaped a bitter harvest on Good Friday, 1939, the day Mussolini ordered his troops to march into Albania. Mussolini wanted Albania to serve as a springboard for an Italian invasion of Greece, which was part of his Mediterranean policy. Resistance by the Albanian army, which had fewer than four thousand men and was largely officered by Italians, collapsed after a few hours. King Zog went into exile for the second time. Mussolini installed a puppet government, and the Albanians once again found themselves under the domination of a foreign invader.

In the middle of World War II, when the alliance between the Axis powers fell apart, the Germans took over control. But the German occupation was never very powerful, and it grew increasingly weak as troops had to be withdrawn to reinforce the German efforts on more important fronts. The number of partisan groups had been increasing, not only because of national hatred of foreign rule, but also as a result of the favorable prospects of independence after the war. The partisans could now operate in comparative safety. On November 29, 1944, even before the war ended, forces of the so-called National Freedom Movement took Tirana. Albania's sovereignty was once more proclaimed. A new epoch in the history of the brave people of the Albanian mountain country had begun.

II

Forebodings of Revolt

IN THE SUMMER OF 1961, as every year, the traditional "Soviet-Albanian Friendship Week" was opened with a mass demonstration attended by the entire corps of Party leaders. From a cloudless sky the sun burned down on the wide boulevards in the center of Tirana. But instead of the quiet that usually marks the midday hour in the Albanian capital, the streets echoed to the sound of masses of people streaming toward Scanderbeg Square, the enormous gathering place in the center of the city. They were of all kinds: workers from the textile and food-processing plants in the southwest, artisans from the north, and officials from the big buildings that house countless bureaucrats. Shabbily dressed working men and women marched alongside well-dressed functionaries, whose solemn countenances testified to their superior standing. Many of them carried flags, placards, or banners. They were on the way to a political demonstration.

The nearer they got to Scanderbeg Square, the more disciplined they became. They began to form groups, falling into step and composing themselves into ranks. Now the social distinctions began to be a little more obvious. The column of bureaucrats and functionaries was marked by white shirts, pants without patches, and good shoes. Even their banners were clean and freshly painted, in contrast to the faded and ill-written placards of the "toiling masses." As the columns reached the square, they were joined by bands: a brass band for the functionaries, and smaller, less impressive ones, consisting of clarinet-like instruments, drums, and tambourines, for the poorer and less important celebrants.

Scanderbeg Square itself was jammed with people, and from among them there projected a forest of boards, flags, and enormous portraits. Everyone's eyes were turned toward a dais, sur-

8

rounded by a semicircular wooden fence, its whitewashed boards displaying two red flags and a huge placard proclaiming "Long Live Soviet-Albanian Friendship."

At last, the sound of automobile engines heralded the arrival of the top Party leaders. Practiced groups began to shout Communist slogans, which were taken up in a kind of chant by the thousands waiting for the program to start.

Finally, the climax was reached. The dictator mounted the dais. All the chants merged into one deafening roar that sounded like a battle cry, "Enver Hoxha! Enver Hoxha!" Hoxha replied with a smile and a patronizing wave of the hand. The members of the Politbureau formed themselves behind him, the ranking dignitaries in the front row, with the Party underlings slipping quietly into their places behind the mighty. While the crowds were still cheering, a man of medium stature took his place on the speaker's rostrum. He was Hysni Kapo, Chairman of the Soviet-Albanian Friendship Society, and the third-ranking man in the Albanian Politbureau. Neither his intelligent features nor his cold eyes behind the rimless glasses revealed the slightest reaction to the frenetic cheering of the people.

The cheering died away and Kapo began his speech. For two hours he eulogized Albanian friendship toward the Soviet people and the great leaders of the Soviet fraternal Party. At appropriate points his speech was interrupted by more cheers and the chanting of Hoxha's name or the words "Marxism-Leninism."

Everything seemed to be going according to the normal pattern of such events in the people's democracies, demonstrating anew the bonds of loyalty to the most important, the mightiest, the paragon of all the Communist parties in the Eastern bloc.

To the attentive observer, however, there were signs of a change of emphasis in the ritual phrases extolling the Communist solidarity. To begin with, there was the extraordinary fact that the speech was not being made by the country's top man, but by one of his minions. Hysni Kapo is undoubtedly an intelligent and wily representative of the leadership of the Albanian Party. He gave proof of his ability in his speech, in which he extolled the achievements of the mighty Soviet ally in a long tirade, without, however, once mentioning the Kremlin's current domestic or foreign-policy line or making a single reference to Nikita Khrushchev.

On the other hand, the speech contained a good deal about "maintaining the purity of Marxism-Leninism," about the perils lurking in the evil of "revisionism," and about the duty to maintain the monolithic unity of the socialist camp. And it was certainly not by chance that the façade of a nearby ministry building displayed only one greater-than-lifesize portrait, that of Albania's own dictator, Enver Hoxha. Nor was it sheer coincidence that the crowd on the dais did not include the official representative of the Soviet Union.

The only one who seemed to be really pleased with the events taking place on the Scanderbeg Square was Josef Vissarionovich Stalin. There he stood on his marble base, behind the crowd and face to face with the mighty ones on the dais. He seemed to be acting as the patron of the meeting, as the symbol of a development that had revealed itself today in a number of small details— small but by no means unimportant.

When the Soviet-Albanian Friendship Week of 1961 opened, I had been in Albania for three weeks. In view of what I had seen and heard in that time, I was not so surprised by the lack of genuine political solidarity, but by the fact that such a demonstration of friendship was possible at all. In the course of my travels through Albania I had come across signs of a new development throughout the country. Even the propaganda in the streets made it plain that dark clouds hung over Albania's alliance with the U.S.S.R. The display windows of the Party offices and Houses of Culture did show pictures of the spacemen Gagarin and Titov, and there was no lack of enthusiasm for window displays on the Soviet Union's technical progress, with models of rockets, sputniks, and spaceships. But what was nowhere to be seen was any documentation of the principle of peaceful coexistence as Moscow understands it. Nor did I once see the name of Khrushchev, who rates as the initiator of the new Communist line associated with the words "peaceful coexistence."

Red China, on the other hand, was given a much bigger propaganda play. The cordial handshake between Mao Tse-tung and Hoxha on Hoxha's arrival in Peking was one of the most important exhibits in the Party display windows in towns and villages everywhere. And this was not the only manifestation of the Albanian attitude toward Red China. There were many montages of Chinese comrades engaged in industrial construction work, in the fields, or doing military exercises. The Albanians had also taken over from the Chinese the slogan "Build up Socialism with the pickaxe in one hand and the rifle in the other," which has now become the country's most important war cry. The Tirana leaders have adopted the same militant political concept as their counterparts in Peking.

What is behind this venturesome alteration of course? Since there is no attempt to conceal this change of heart, even in official propaganda, I felt justified in putting the question to every Albanian official to whom I spoke. Their answers varied. Most of them shied away from this delicate subject. They began to answer in monosyllables and made every effort to change the subject. But occasionally one or the other would let something slip. From the patchwork of discussions and conversations it began to emerge that Albania's coolness toward Moscow and cordiality toward Peking was no sudden or precipitate happening, but rather a slow and gradual process. The first indications of the impending change occurred in the spring of 1960.

Defiance in Tirana

It was in April, 1960, that the world was given its first glimpse of the long-threatened split in the relations between the countries of the Eastern bloc. Peking used the celebrations marking the ninetieth anniversary of Lenin's birth to launch an attack on the leading position hitherto held by the Kremlin in world Communism. In speeches and articles, the men around Mao Tse-tung demanded a more aggressive and orthodox alternative to the theses and guiding principles on the "genuinely Leninist" home and foreign policies proclaimed by Moscow. The Kremlin had to take up the challenge. Hitherto it had looked as if the Chinese were out to conduct a campaign of pinpricks in an indirect attack on certain basic principles laid down by the Soviet center; annoying, perhaps, but not actually dangerous. But now, having come into the open, the Chinese were posing a serious threat to the Soviet claim to be the absolute authority. A controversy began that continued through most of 1960.

At this same time, when the rebellious attitude of the Chinese Communists toward Moscow hit the headlines, it began to appear that the Albanian leaders were no longer willing to follow the Moscow line unconditionally. The first indication of this attitude came when Tirana, after something of an inner struggle, cautiously and circumspectly adopted an attitude of approval toward certain domestic concepts voiced by the Chinese ideologists. Mao's People's Communes and the slogan about the "great leap forward"—both of which Peking had declared to be fundamental to the structure of its governmental system—were received with benevolent approval in Albania.

Tirana also caused comment by some of its views on foreign affairs. In April, 1960, shortly before the eagerly awaited Paris Summit Conference, the entire Eastern bloc opened a massive campaign in support of an easing of international tension. For the first time, Albania got out of line when Ramiz Alia, a prominent Communist leader, made a speech in which he drew a direct parallel between the "treason" of the Yugoslav revisionists and the Kremlin's efforts to bring about a universal easing of tension. Western observers of the Sino-Soviet controversy pricked up their ears. It suddenly seemed worthwhile to pay attention not only to the statements emanating from Moscow and Peking, but also to those from Tirana. The pocket-sized country of Albania, for more than ten years a Cinderella among the satellites, suddenly became interesting. In view of the altercation between the Russians and the Chinese, the material published by the Albanian Communists now would also have to be studied.

In June, 1960, the Albanian Communists removed all possible doubt about their attitude. Khrushchev had taken advantage of the Rumanian Party Congress in Bucharest to call a meeting of the ranking Communists of the Eastern bloc, to resolve the controversy between Moscow and Peking the way he wanted. While all the important Party leaders of the East European Communist camp showed up, the Chinese thought it unnecessary to send top members of their Party hierarchy to represent them. The Albanians did the same. It was not Enver Hoxha, the head of the Albanian Communist Party, who went to Bucharest to sit alongside his colleagues from Moscow's other satellites. Nor was it even the second man in the Albanian Party, Prime Minister Mehmet Shehu, but only the third man in line, Hysni Kapo. Kapo was certainly a member of the Albanian Politbureau and a particularly close confidant of Enver Hoxha, but he still did not possess nearly the authority and power appropriate to the head of a delegation to an Eastern summit meeting.

It was not only in the externals that the Albanians followed the Chinese example in Bucharest. Hysni Kapo also followed in the footsteps of the Chinese in respect to political tactics. Neither the Chinese nor the Albanians indulged in recriminations against the Soviet Party leaders. Exactly like his colleague from Peking, Kapo affirmed the unity of the Communist camp and confirmed Albanian acceptance of the leading role of the Soviet Union. On the controversy between Moscow and Peking, however, Kapo, in striking contrast to the other satellite leaders, said not a word.

Kapo's speech played down such matters as "peaceful coexistence" and "the inevitability of wars." And there was no mention of "dogmatists" or "sectarians," on whom the satellite leaders particularly trained their sights. Instead, Kapo poured out vehement abuse on the "revisionists" within the ranks of the Communist movement.

In the months that followed, the pro-Chinese course taken by the Albanian Communists became more and more evident. Speeches, newspaper articles, and radio talks eulogized the correctness of Chinese domestic and foreign policies, and fully supported Peking in the struggle to maintain the "purity of the Marxist-Leninist teaching." All this was accompanied by furious vituperation of the Yugoslav "revisionists." This anti-Belgrade campaign by the Chinese and Albanian Communists was nothing new, of course, but it contrasted strangely with the political propaganda line being put out by the Soviet Union and the other satellite countries, who were working feverishly to justify Khrushchev's foreign policy, without involving Tito.

During that period, strange things happened in Albania. At the beginning of September, 1960, Liri Belishova, the only woman member of the Politbureau, and Kochi Tashko, the chairman of the Central Revision Committee, were expelled from the Party. Belishova was charged with having made "serious mistakes" in the course of her Party political activities, and Tashko was even accused of "hostile activity." At first, the purges among the highest ranks in the Party baffled Western observers of the Albanian scene, for it had been Belishova who had taken up such a decidedly pro-Chinese position in public during the preceding weeks. Belishova was succeeded by Ramiz Alia. Until then, Alia had been nothing more than a candidate for a position in the Politbureau and was generally regarded as pro-Soviet. To complete the confusion, the first accusations and reproaches against these Party leaders were made by Rita Marko, who had just returned from an extended trip to the Soviet Union. For the tiny group of experts on Albanian affairs there could be only one conclusion: something sensational was about to break. By all appearances, Enver Hoxha had seen the light and was getting ready to revert to the old familiar course of traditional devotion to Moscow.

Yet nothing happened to confirm these speculations. What would have been a reliable indication of impending political change anywhere in the Communist world did not seem to hold true in Albania. Tirana remained faithful to the Peking line.

In my conversations with Albanian functionaries, I tried to bring up the cases of Belishova and Tashko, and I always asked the same question: What was the real background story to the expulsion from the Party of these two functionaries? Oddly enough, there was never any attempt to evade the question. No matter to whom I spoke, I was always assured that Belishova and Tashko had never made any secret of their pro-Soviet leanings, and that they had maintained their attitude long after the decision had been made to move closer to Peking's general line. Their stubborn attitude was bound to lead to their expulsion from the Party and to their being relieved of all their offices.

Another incident had even more obscure motives and background. Enver Hoxha ordered the arrest of several army officers and Party functionaries, men who were hardly known abroad, but who were occupying relatively important positions. Among them were the former commander of the Albanian Navy, Rear-Admiral

Teme Sejko; the District Chairman of Elbasan, Tahir Demi; Major-General Halim Jello and two other senior officers; and Adem Osmane, a prominent trade-union leader. Later, at the Fourth Party Congress in February, 1961, when Hoxha made the arrests public for the first time, the allegation was that these men, together with the "Yugoslav revisionists," the Greek monarcho-fascists, and the United States Sixth Fleet, had tried to bring about a *coup d'état* in Albania.

The simultaneousness of the actions—on the one hand, the expulsion of two prominent Party leaders, and on the other, the arrests of important personalities in leading positions in the Albanian state—let loose a flood of speculation and surmise. Taken at their face value, the reasons for the arrests were patently absurd, but there was a possibility that some sort of *Putsch* had been in preparation. There were rumors that the Soviets had had something to do with it, their aim having been to get rid of Enver Hoxha and Mehmet Shehu. The trial, which was staged, literally and metaphorically, in the partisans' mess in Tirana in May, 1961, produced no evidence of such a connection. For one thing, only the men arrested in August and September, 1960, were brought to trial, not Belishova and Tashko. Also, the proceedings—the propaganda purpose of which was underlined by the presence on the opening day of a number of prominent functionaries, such as President Haji Lleshi and Foreign Minister Behar Shtylla—did not give the slightest indication that the Soviets had been implicated in the "conspiracy." According to the indictment, the revolution was to have been brought about in the fall of 1960, by means of armed risings followed by intervention from outside the country. According to the testimony of Tahir Demi, one of the accused, groups of Albanian refugees "trained in Yugoslavia" were to attack in the north of the country under the personal command of Panayot Plaku. Major-General Panayot Plaku, formerly a member of the Albanian Central Committee and Minister without Portfolio, had fled to Yugoslavia in May, 1957. According to the indictment, he was to have formed the new government when the *Putsch* had been successfully carried out.

The state's attorney, on the conclusion of the "evidence" and the testimony of the witnesses, claimed in his closing address that the conspiracy had been intended all along "to furnish agents of foreign powers with military, economic, and other information." Greek and Yugoslav troops were to have covered the armed revolt, while the United States Sixth Fleet was to have intervened from the seaward side. On this last point, Demi made some grotesque claims. One of them was that the task of the Sixth Fleet was "to bombard the Albanian coast and establish communications with the various groups fighting inland."

It would be easy enough to ridicule the phantasmagoria presented by a judicial system working in strict accordance with Stalinist principles. What is more difficult is to determine the truth behind this "treason trial." Who were the real instigators and organizers of the intended *Putsch?* Is it possible that the real purpose was, by the very absurdity of the allegations of collaboration between Greek and Yugoslav troops with the U.S. Sixth Fleet, to lead the knowledgeable to look elsewhere and thus arouse suspicion of Moscow's complicity? The true background to the trial has still not been revealed. And it is strange that, apart from the Bulgarian trade-union paper *Trud,* not a single satellite newspaper reported the trial. Moreover, Enver Hoxha later claimed on several occasions that the Soviets had tried to put direct military pressure on the Albanian leaders. Nevertheless, it is still possible that Hoxha's actions in expelling prominent Communists from the Party and arresting important officers and functionaries were less the result of Soviet machinations than a form of political prophylaxis, intended to forestall any possible contingency.

Meanwhile, the Tirana leaders had not missed the opportunity to provoke their Soviet allies in another matter. In September, 1960, Nikita Khrushchev, together with the leaders of all the satellite Communist Parties, boarded the *Baltica* for a journey to New York, where he intended to take part in the General Assembly of the United Nations. Once again, the Albanian Party leader ostentatiously stayed at home. There may have been good domestic reasons for this, in view of the wave of purges and arrests. However, it was curious that less than three months after he had failed to attend the meeting of satellite Party leaders in Bucharest, Hoxha once again refused the chance of conferring with his colleagues of the East European fraternal Parties. His place in New York was

taken by the Prime Minister, Mehmet Shehu, but even he declined
the opportunity of a leisurely cruise on the *Baltica* and travelled
by air. Khrushchev and his companions obviously regarded the attitude of Hoxha and his Prime Minister as a calculated affront. At
least this was what Shehu was made to feel in New York. Whereas
Khrushchev had a number of much publicized conferences with
the "arch-revisionist" and "deadly enemy" of Albania, Tito, he
showed the Albanian Prime Minister the cold shoulder. This attitude was faithfully aped by the other Communist leaders, who
also made a point of cutting the number-two man in the Albanian
Party hierarchy.

If anyone was still skeptical of the Albanian change of course,
events during the latter part of November, 1960, must have persuaded even the most unbelieving. The Moscow celebrations
marking the anniversary of the October Revolution were followed
by a conference of the Eighty-One Communist Parties. It had
taken a long time for Hoxha to come out with it, but his explanation of why he had not attended the Bucharest meeting in June
was that since a discussion of the internal differences within the
Eastern bloc had not originally been intended, his presence was
not necessary. This time the situation was quite different. This
time all concerned knew in advance that not only was there to be a
full-scale discussion of these differences, but that the main item
on the agenda was to be the controversy between Moscow and
Peking.

The importance Peking attached to this meeting was attested
to by the strength of the delegation the Chinese sent to Moscow.
Their team was led by the second man in the Red Chinese Government, Liu Shao Chi. He was backed up by Teng Hsiao Ping,
the General Secretary of the Chinese Communist Party, and Peng
Chen, a member of the Chinese Politbureau, who had been handling internal Eastern-bloc problems since the Bucharest meeting.

Albania was correspondingly strongly represented. Enver
Hoxha headed the delegation, which included Mehmet Shehu
and Hysni Kapo. The other member was Ramiz Alia, a rising star
in the Albanian Party machine, who was being given a chance to
win his spurs.

Few details of the discussions during the November meeting

have become known in the West. The only information that did leak out concerned the attitude of the Albanian Communists. There is not much doubt that these leaks, presumably from an unofficial but reliable source, were deliberately launched by the Kremlin and spread by the Kremlin's Communist allies with the intention of discrediting the Albanian leaders.

It emerged from these deliberate leaks that Hoxha unconditionally supported the Chinese challenge to Moscow. The Albanian leader, one of the bitterest and most convinced critics of the Kremlin's policies, heaped reproaches on Khrushchev. On November 16, he gave a speech to the representatives of international Communism in which he did not mince words. On every disputed point, Hoxha supported the Chinese view. He said that in August, 1960, the Soviet leaders had demanded that the Albanian Party throw its weight on the side of Moscow against Peking. When this demand was not met, Khrushchev decided to bring about the fall of the existing Party leadership by intriguing against it in the Albanian Party and in the Army. Hoxha went on to say that the Soviet Defense Minister, Marshal Malinovski, had severely criticized Albania at a Warsaw Pact Conference. The Soviet Marshal Gretchko, who was appointed Commander-in-Chief of the Warsaw Pact forces in replacement of Marshal Koniev in June, 1960, had threatened Albania with exclusion from the Warsaw Pact. Hoxha hinted that Khrushchev was even thinking of having Albania thrown out of the "socialist camp."

To round this all off, Hoxha claimed that the Kremlin had tried to put pressure on the Tirana leaders by deliberately withholding promised wheat shipments. In 1960, Albania had suffered earthquakes, floods, and a drought, and was in danger of mass starvation. The country's stocks of wheat would have lasted only for fifteen days. In the end, Moscow had agreed to deliver 10,000 tons (instead of the promised 50,000). Furthermore, there had been delays in the delivery of even this reduced amount, and the wheat did not reach Albania until September and October.

Even before the international Communist meeting, Moscow must have realized what the Albanian attitude was going to be. It has been reported that as early as November 6, before the conference began, Khrushchev said, "Russia has lost an Albania and the People's Republic of China has gained an Albania." Even so, the Soviet leader had not expected such tirades from the Albanian Communists. He could hardly have been prepared for the torrent of bitter, personal abuse that was contained in Hoxha's speech before the assembled delegates. This accounted for the anger with which Khrushchev reacted to Hoxha's attack: "Comrade Hoxha, you have poured a bucket of filth over me; you are going to have to wash it off again." What Khrushchev had in mind to do to the rebellious comrades in Tirana is evident from a remark he made to the General Secretary of the Chinese Party, Hsiao Ping; "We shall deal with Albania the way we dealt with Yugoslavia."

However, the Kremlin hesitated to translate the Soviet leader's furious words into deeds, believing that there was still a possibility of making the recalcitrant Albanian leadership see reason. Official quarters remained silent on the subject of the Albanian outburst at the conference. There has only been one official Party statement on the behavior of the Albanians at the Moscow summit conference, made by the head of the East German Socialist Unity Party, Walter Ulbricht. At a plenary meeting of the East German Communist Party on December 15, 1960, Ulbricht claimed that the Albanians had revealed a "dogmatic and sectarian" attitude in Moscow. This was a very mild description of what actually had happened. Nevertheless, that such a rebuke to a brother Party should be uttered in public at all was not only sensational—it was without parallel in the history of the Communist movement.

Hoxha and Shehu left Moscow unexpectedly a week before the conclusion of the conference. From then on, developments in the relations between Soviet Russia and Albania took their irrevocable course. While there was a noticeable easing-off in the open altercation between China and the Soviet Union after December, 1960, the controversy between Moscow and Tirana grew more acute. Hoxha did nothing to propitiate Moscow, and the Soviets were obliged to give notice of their displeasure. A plain indication of this was the form in which Moscow couched its New Year wishes to the Albanian comrades. The Kremlin carefully avoided using the usual opening formulation, "Dear Comrades," and confined itself to greetings and good wishes "to the fraternal Albanian people." Those familiar with Moscow's official Party linguistics knew that this was equivalent to placing the Albanian Party leaders on the same level as their "arch-enemies," the "revisionist" Yugoslav leaders headed by Tito.

Nevertheless, there were signs that Moscow was still willing to make one more attempt to improve relations with Tirana before the Fourth Albanian Party Congress, which had been postponed until February, 1961. Shortly after the Red summit conference in November, the Soviets nominated a new ambassador to Albania. This was Shikin, a former general in the headquarters of the Red Army's political administration. According to Western information, Shikin had played some dark role in the Korean war, and in recent years had held the important position of deputy head of the Cadre Section of the Soviet Central Committee. He possessed a number of qualities that seemed to fit him for the task of exerting gentle pressure on the men around Enver Hoxha, to urge them back into the Soviet fold.

Simultaneous with this new appointment, the Kremlin started another maneuver. As 1961 began, the satellite states that were faithful to Moscow began to dangle the bait of trade treaties before the eyes of the Albanian leaders. The Soviet Union, Rumania, and East Germany made tempting offers, the East Germans going so far as to suggest expanding the volume of trade by 55 per cent in 1961.

It began to look as though there really was a chance of doing business with the Albanians. In a speech to the Tirana Party Committee on January 6, 1961, Hoxha praised the Soviet Union as he had not done for a long time. He even managed to say that "dogmatism" and "sectarianism" must be dealt with as a matter of urgency. Prime Minister Mehmet Shehu said much the same in a speech in Koritza.

However, the saying that "one swallow does not make a summer" applied to Albania, for the cautious steps toward reconciliation did not lead very far. On January 8, a powerful Albanian economic delegation boarded a plane for China. There was an exchange of personal telegrams between Hoxha and Mao Tse-tung that gave a fair idea of what was in the wind. The course of the proceedings at the impending Fourth Albanian Party Congress had been finally determined, and Moscow was forced to realize that its last-minute effort to effect a change of heart in Tirana had failed.

The Fourth Congress, which took place in February, clearly confirmed that the Albanian leaders had not budged an inch since November, 1960. Hoxha and Shehu reaffirmed their intention to resist any pressure from the Soviets, and made no bones that they expected the backing of China. The Albanian leader and his most important associates were prepared to concede the leading role of the Soviet Union in the socialist camp, but they still severely criticized the methods used by the Soviet leaders. They stubbornly rejected Moscow's accusations that the Albanian Communists were "dogmatists," and Shehu disingenuously expressed his opinion that only revisionists could say such a thing. The Albanian Party cadre, he maintained, consisted of "unsullied Marxists," who were "unshakable in their faith to the bitter end." Furthermore, they would never tolerate allegations that Lenin's teachings were "out-of-date" and "needed revising." The Albanians were not in the habit of calling the enemies of the nation "friends," as the revisionists did. Anyone who trifled with established Leninist concepts the way the revisionists were doing, he contended, would inevitably find that he had loaded himself with a Trojan horse. The Albanian leaders had not the slightest intention of following along this path.

What Shehu had said in these few sentences was nothing more nor less than a direct shaft aimed at the arguments the Soviet leader had put up at the Bucharest meeting six months earlier.

Hoxha's remarks were no less forceful than those of the Prime Minister. The Albanian Communists, he declared, had always possessed "the correct Marxist-Leninist insight" into the basic political conditions of the current era. The "correct insight" turned out to be the one that coincided with the point of view of the Chinese comrades. Hoxha illustrated the point by means of a number of examples. The Chinese influence in back of his assertion that peace could not be assured by making concessions to the imperialists, or by singing their praises, was fairly obvious. Moreover, Hoxha went on, since the forces of international reaction had encircled the Eastern bloc with "three hundred military bases," what was the point of all this nonsense about the alleged willingness of the imperialist powers to disarm and talk peace? President Kennedy, who had just taken office, was in Hoxha's view just as untrustworthy as his predecessor, Eisenhower. To the joy of Peking and to the annoyance of Moscow, Hoxha concluded the foreign policy section of his statement with the demand that the Chinese People's Republic must be represented at all future summit conferences on international policy.

The Albanian leaders could not have given plainer evidence of their pro-Chinese course or issued a more open challenge to the Kremlin. *Pravda* accordingly made drastic cuts in its published version of Hoxha's speech to the Albanian Party Congress, and deleted all the radical parts and the utterances distasteful to Moscow. The Soviet reader was not allowed to learn anything about Hoxha's opinion on the necessity to "maintain the purity of Marxist-Leninist teaching" or of "the uselessness of making peace with the Imperialists."

It was in vain that the Soviet Communists had sent Pospelov, one of their cleverest and best-equipped ideological experts, to the Albanian congress. Pospelov did indeed give his Albanian comrades an urgent warning against "leftist deviationist tendencies," but it was without effect. The other delegates from countries loyal to the Moscow line also did their best to support Moscow's viewpoint. Roman Novak, a member of the Polish Politbureau, pointed out to the assembled Albanian delegates that the Leninist policy of peaceful coexistence had gained the Kremlin the sympathy not only of the liberated Afro-Asian peoples, but of all other neutral states. The Albanian Party leaders, however, remained unimpressed by the Polish testimony, which also contained a veiled criticism of the Chinese and Albanian leaders. Following the same journalistic principle as *Pravda*, the Albanian radio and press reports did not contain those passages in which the leader of the Polish delegation had called for a policy of peaceful coexistence.

The delegates to the congress confirmed both Hoxha and Shehu in their positions in the Party, and the leading functionaries seemed to be solidly behind their leaders. For Moscow, the final outcome of the Fourth Party Congress in Tirana meant a worsening rather than an improvement of the situation in the Eastern bloc.

The congress was followed by new skirmishes between Moscow and Tirana. The Albanian security authorities arrested two officials of the Albanian Foreign Ministry who were alleged to have given the Soviet embassy in Tirana access to secret notes and confidential minutes of the Party Congress. From that time on, the staff of the Soviet embassy in the Albanian capital was kept under permanent, strict surveillance.

In March, 1961, a conference of member states of the Warsaw Pact was called. As usual, it was attended by the Party leaders of all the East European people's democracies. Once again, Albania was only represented by second-string functionaries. There is a good deal of evidence that an important decision regarding Albania was taken at this Warsaw Pact meeting. Moscow's patience was exhausted and Khrushchev mobilized all the other satellite Communist parties for the counterblow. It looked as if the Soviets were no longer prepared to tolerate any further provocation by the Albanian leaders without taking appropriate action. Moscow had finally decided to act.

The Lonely Army

One of the most surprising measures taken by Moscow against Tirana was the withdrawal of Soviet naval units from Albania. At the beginning of June, 1961, Western observation posts reported that a Soviet submarine flotilla had left the Mediterranean via Gibraltar. This unit, eight submarines and a modern supply ship, was sighted in the Atlantic and later in the North Sea. There could be no doubt about it—the Soviet submarine flotilla had left its forward naval base on the Adriatic coast of Albania, and was returning to its home bases on the Baltic.

At first, Western military circles did not attach much importance to this Soviet naval move. They were unwilling as yet to believe that the Soviets were withdrawing their naval units from Albania completely. It seemed improbable that the Moscow military planners would relinquish their only naval base in the Mediterranean, particularly since this base had caused the United States Sixth Fleet, a pillar of the Western defense strategy, a great deal of uneasiness. At this stage, therefore, the general belief was that the move of the Soviet submarines was nothing more than the relief of individual units, which would shortly be replaced by new, perhaps much more modern forces.

In the summer and early fall of 1961, when I was in Albania, the problem of the background to the move of the Soviet submarines was still a mystery. Unexpectedly, I received permission to make a trip to the restricted military area of the Valona naval base and its island outpost, Sasseno. Astonished as I was at the decision of the Albanian authorities, I was less surprised than the East German representatives in Tirana, who, I was told, had long been refused permission to visit Valona. The question that naturally arose in my mind was whether my trip to Valona had been approved in order to demonstrate that there were no longer any Soviet naval units stationed in Albania's "strategic center." If this *was* the Albanian intention, it succeeded completely.

The harbor of Valona lies some distance outside the town itself. From my seat on the terrace of a small inn, I could see the whole area of the port—perhaps the word "port" is a slight exaggeration, for neither in size nor extent could Valona outdo many a small European fishing village. Opposite Valona and a short distance from it lies the island of Sasseno. If Valona had not lived up to my mental picture of it, neither did Sasseno, which, small and squat, looked like a clump of rock hunched in the sea.

The bay of Valona made the same uninspiring impression. There was no question of anything that could be called marine traffic. Only a few rowing boats rocked on the Adriatic swell. In the middle of the bay, a ship's mast could be seen sticking up out of the water, with a small red warning light at the top. According to my Albanian escort, this ship was sunk by the Italians during their bombing attack on Albania in 1939, and it was still lying where it sank.

This explanation made nonsensical many of the rumors and analyses by Western military experts. The mysterious bay of Valona, the harbor, and the island outpost of Sasseno—these had all been the subject of earnest speculation in the West. Here in this bay, lying directly on the fifty-mile-wide Strait of Otranto, a whole fleet could ride at anchor, it had been said; and the Soviets thus had an operational base in the Mediterranean that might well become a deciding factor in the world-wide East-West conflict. Reports claimed that submarine pens had been blasted out of the cliffs, and that they harbored a permanent force of twelve Soviet B-class submarines and two supply vessels. The potential capacity of the base was said to be much greater than this, however, and more than fifty submarines could be accommodated in the bay of Valona. Another rumor spoke of two Soviet Admirals being permanently stationed in Albania. They were supposed to be subordinated to the Black Sea Fleet and to enjoy wide operational freedom of action. Some Western experts claimed to have information that the Soviet submarines spent eight to ten hours a week at sea and were combined at regular intervals for extensive maneuvers.

The Soviets, it was also claimed, had taken over from the Italians an advanced system of bases on Sasseno, so that between them Valona and Sasseno formed a "Red Gibraltar" on the Adriatic, from which the most northerly-reaching arm of the Mediterranean could be sealed off and blocked. The dreaded possibility of a Soviet advance into the reaches of the Mediterranean had, it was argued, thus been realized. Whereas the Turks controlled the access to the Black Sea and the Soviets could be bottled up in case of trouble, the situation in Albania meant that the Soviets had pushed forward to the very heart of the Mediterranean complex. Here, too, Europe's south flank was menaced by the military might of Russia. Albania's role as Russia's strategic outpost in this potentially explosive area of world politics could not be taken seriously enough. This was the general burden of many perfectly serious military opinions in the West.

Judged by what I was able to see in Valona, such far-reaching conclusions were, to say the least, exaggerated. It cannot be denied that after 1948, the Russians did take a certain amount of trouble to try to gain a military foothold on the Mediterranean coast, but their efforts were cautious and limited. Moscow also made an attempt to modernize the Albanian fighting forces, which had hardly been much above the level of guerrilla bands until then. Military equipment and tanks were provided for purposes of local defense, and the Albanians were presented with about a dozen airplanes. The navy was built up to the point where it possessed motor torpedo boats, minesweepers, and escort vessels. Until recently, however, according to reliable information, the Albanian Navy never consisted of more than four subchasers, six minesweepers, and a few smaller units. Members of the Albanian Navy and Air Force went to the Soviet Union for training, and ships of the Soviet Black Sea and Baltic fleets paid regular "friendship visits" to Albanian ports, in which the Soviets set up a number of supply bases. But these were never anything more than small auxiliary depots. No regular Soviet military forces were ever stationed in Albania.

It was probably not much different with the legendary Soviet submarine forces in Albania. Russian subs have only been appearing on the Albanian coast since 1958, and serious Western observers believe that there were never more than ten stationed in Albanian waters at any one time.

Artillery units were stationed on the island of Sasseno, and a few shelters were built there for smaller ships, but geographical considerations alone preclude the possibility of affording shelter to a fleet of any size in wartime. The narrow Valona Bay offers no possibility of deploying a fleet for safety against atomic attack, nor are there space or facilities for carrying out repairs. The island of Sasseno does not even have its own supply of drinking water, and it is not surprising that the Soviet submarine flotilla on the Adriatic coast was always accompanied by substantial supply units. From the beginning, the restricted logistical facilities must have made the Soviets realize the inadvisability of any very large-scale strategic experimenting in Albania.

There was still another reason for the Kremlin's caution: Political conditions in Albania did not offer sufficient protection to an extremely costly military setup. There was too much prestige at stake. The Kremlin has never displayed the degree of confidence in the Albanian Communist leaders that it has shown toward the other satellites nearer to the territory of the Soviet Union. The deciding factor in the Soviet Union's strategic thinking may well have been the fact that Albania is the only one of the satellites that is geographically isolated from the Eastern bloc. The land supply lines could be easily cut in time of war, and the sea routes would be even riskier. The Soviets therefore seemed to be concerned merely with giving some sort of a demonstration of their military presence in Albania. The Kremlin could be certain that this presence, even in the form of weak and strategically unimportant elements, would still cause Western military staffs serious disquiet.

The considerations that justify a skeptical evaluation of the reports of Soviet naval bases in Albania apply even more to the legend that the Soviet Union set up rocket bases in the Albanian mountains. Reports to this effect have cropped up at regular intervals in the Western press during recent years, and Moscow was only too anxious to have them believed. During his journey through Albania in the summer of 1959, Khrushchev himself repeatedly stressed the value of Albania in the Kremlin's strategic planning. In order to give his words added force, he brought Defense Minister Malinovski with him. Khrushchev said that Albania was "exceptionally suitable" for the setting up of rocket bases. The height of the mountains and the depth of the valleys, according to Khrushchev, were particularly favorable for resisting the attack of an enemy "threatening the Socialist countries with his rockets."

As in so many instances, Khrushchev's words were nothing more than a threat, with no real military basis to support it. The same considerations that led the Soviets to confine their naval capacity to an *acte de présence*, kept them from actually setting up rocket bases in Albania. The country's geographical and domestic situation, plus the extended and vulnerable supply lines from the Soviet Union to the Adriatic, seemed too dangerous for Moscow's liking.

This analysis is important for the assessment of the Soviet measures against Albania in the military sphere. In pulling its naval units out of Albania, the Soviet Union had not in fact surrendered a trump card it might have played against the West, as is sometimes maintained in Western analyses of the move. The Soviet countermeasures were primarily directed against the rebellious Albanian leaders. The presence of Soviet naval forces had given them a feeling of security: It not only was an indication that Moscow regarded Albania as a useful member of the Warsaw Pact community, but it kept the Soviet Union more closely tied to its military commitments. In ordering the withdrawal of its forces, the Soviet Union had made it perfectly plain to the Tirana leaders that Albania's status as a member of the Eastern bloc's military alliance had become rather shaky. To the men in Moscow, the unmistakeable warning that the Kremlin thus gave to Tirana was more important than the artificial anxiety the presence of Soviet forces might have caused to the Western nations. The Soviets could manage without Albania's membership of the Warsaw Pact. The leaders in Tirana, however, felt very differently.

The psychological effect achieved by the Soviet Union in withdrawing their submarine flotilla from Albania was considerable. A symbol of brotherhood-in-arms was destroyed. Both the leaders of the Albanian army and the top men in the political sphere were uneasy.

Another military measure taken by the Soviets probably had even greater practical consequences. In the early summer of 1961, the training of all Albanian officers, cadets, and noncoms in the Soviet Union or the East European satellite countries was brought to a stop. Since then, there has been not a single Albanian studying at a military academy in the Eastern bloc. It has been impossible, therefore, for the Tirana Government to keep its army up-to-date on military theory. The importance of this fact should not be underrated. The Albanian soldier is a courageous fighter, as he has proved often in the past centuries; but in modern warfare, it is no longer personal bravery alone that counts. Training and technical know-how are equally important, and this is where the Albanian Army seems to lag behind.

Diplomatic and Cultural Isolation

The rage and bitterness felt by the Albanians as a result of the Russian reprisals in the military sphere were understandable. It was not long before rumors began to be heard in Warsaw that when the Soviets were in the process of withdrawing their submarine fleet from Valona, the Albanians had seized some Soviet vessels and stubbornly refused to hand them back to the Soviets. Almost a year later, an Austrian Communist functionary named Fürnberg confirmed this rumor, when he publicly stated in Vienna that Albania really had illegally taken control of several Soviet ships. In spite of this, however, these reports should be treated with reserve. The Albanians are admittedly capable of doing this sort of thing, but, on the other hand, Moscow is out to blacken the recalcitrant Albanian comrades by any method that presents itself and to justify its own behavior. For this reason, it would probably be advisable to employ the same degree of skepticism toward this alleged act of piracy as toward the Soviet's subsequent claim that they had been obliged to withdraw their naval force from Albania because Albania had "greatly harmed the Warsaw Pact states' defense effort." The real reasons for the military reprisals against Albania were in fact purely political.

Shortly after the departure of the Soviet submarines, the Albanian leaders took further steps. They declared the military attaché in the Soviet embassy in Tirana *persona non grata*. This promptly led to a series of countermeasures. The Kremlin immediately reduced the size of its embassy staff, and took steps to see that all the satellite embassies in Tirana followed suit. German technicians in Albania told me that the staff of the East German embassy in Tirana was also drastically cut. Until then, the permanent staff of the embassy had been twenty, but in the early summer of 1961, it was reduced to twelve. It is significant, even if not surprising, that the East German military attaché was one of those who disappeared.

The Albanians did not let matters rest there. The severe measures of control, to which hitherto only the Western embassy staffs (the Italians and the French) and the Yugoslav legation had been subjected, were now extended to all the Communist states' embassies except that of China. The official version gave, of course, a different reason for this step. It will be remembered that shortly after the Fourth Party Congress, two foreign ministry officials were arrested, allegedly for letting the Soviet embassy have access to internal notes and minutes of the Party Congress. But even this explanation left no doubt about the minatory character of the new measures of control.

Toward visitors from the West, the members of the satellite embassies maintained a tight-lipped attitude regarding the nature and extent of the surveillance to which they were subjected. This is understandable, since things have not yet reached the point where the Communists are willing to "wash their dirty linen" before a capitalist public. Nevertheless, the faces of the Eastern-bloc diplomats reveal the effort it costs them to conceal their anger at their Albanian allies. Yugoslav diplomats, on the other hand, are much more frank about the "control" being exercised by the Albanian security authorities. It may be that the Titoist "arch-enemies" have suffered more than anyone else as a result of the increased severity of the surveillance. However, in view of the state of the political game, and the barely concealed fury of the Albanian functionaries at their Soviet and satellite comrades, the surveillance of the Moscow-line embassies is probably almost as strictly carried out.

Reports by Yugoslav representatives on their being shadowed by the Tirana security authorities throw an interesting light on the mentality of the Albanian leaders. Each member of the embassy staff has one or two—or, in some cases, three—permanent Albanian escorts. If a Yugoslav diplomat goes into a shop, he will find one of his escorts at his side while he makes his purchases. If he goes to see a doctor or into a hospital, he will have an escort at least as far as the door. Sometimes the security official will even follow him into the waiting room, opening the door of the consulting room from time to time to check that no subversive activities are going on during the doctor's examination. In the café, in the theater, and at official receptions, the Yugoslav diplomats' escorts are always there, always at the diplomats' elbows at any point where they might come into contact with an Albanian citizen. The Yugoslavs cannot shake off their escorts even on the beach. The shadowers go with them into the water and come out the minute their charges do. If the diplomat sunbathes, his escort will be keeping him company from a short distance away, never getting nearer and never going away. The escorts never make the slightest effort to conceal their presence; indeed, they give the impression that they want to be noticed.

There are always several cars belonging to the Albanian security service parked next door to the Yugoslav embassy. The minute a Yugoslav car moves off, one of these escort cars falls in behind it, and stays behind it at an invariable distance of ten to fifteen yards. After nightfall, this distance is cut down and the Yugoslav car is kept in the glare of undimmed headlights. Sometimes, in particularly "suspicious" cases, the Yugoslav car will be tagged by two cars, although this will usually depend on the number of passengers in the Yugoslav car. Where this does happen, one of the Albanian cars will take up its position in front of the Yugoslavs, and will thus dictate the speed. The cars will stop or brake without any apparent reason, depending solely on what the secret police driver thinks is necessary for effective surveillance.

The Yugoslav diplomats can also tell much about the difficulties foreign embassies have with other matters, such as staff, servants, etc. As in all countries behind the Iron Curtain, the welfare of embassy staffs is looked after by the "Office of Diplomatic Services." Since the middle of 1961, this office has become one of the biggest trials the diplomats have to bear. If a Yugoslav diplomat wants to have his shoes repaired, he must first apply to the "Office of Diplomatic Services," because no Albanian shoemaker is allowed to repair the shoes of a "revisionist" without official authority. It is no longer possible for a member of the Yugoslav diplomatic staff to go directly to a hospital for medical treatment. He must first apply to the "Office." When the child of a Yugoslav diplomat one day fell seriously ill, the Albanian doctor contacted refused to accept the patient immediately, in spite of all entreaties from the embassy.

The work of the foreign embassies is made difficult in other ways, too. For example, the Yugoslav embassy's official interpreter was suddenly removed by the Albanian authorities in May, 1961. Inquiries at the "Office of Diplomatic Services" were met with the announcement that the interpreter was ill, and furthermore that he was no longer willing to work for the embassy. When the matter was referred to a higher authority, the Foreign Ministry just stopped giving any replies. At the same time, the Russian language teacher, who used to give lessons to several members of the embassy staff, failed to show up at the appointed hours. Once again the "Office" gave the terse reply that the lady had fallen ill. When the embassy gardener quit his job, the "Office" refused to provide a driver for an embassy car. Then all the Albanian hired help disappeared overnight without leaving any message, and the "Office" declined to find substitutes. The Yugoslav embassy staff then realized what was meant by "more rigorous control measures" over the foreign embassies.

These measures made themselves especially felt in the shape of new methods which make all normal routine business almost impossible. The Yugoslav embassy was hardly able to maintain contact with its own nationals living in Albania. No Yugoslav was allowed to enter the embassy, even for the handling of consular business; indeed, the militiaman on duty at the entrance to the embassy would allow nobody in. The embassy cannot even keep in touch with Yugoslav nationals by letter or in any other way. Letters are invariably returned, stamped "addressee unknown."

Should a Yugoslav diplomat in Tirana take a notion to make a quick trip to his homeland, whose border is only a hundred miles or so from the Albanian capital, he must apply for a visa twenty-four hours in advance. The visa is valid for one month, but it will only allow the holder to cross the frontier when presented in conjunction with an exit permit issued by the Albanian frontier police. But this exit permit is only valid for one day. If the Yugoslav diplomat should be unable to reach the frontier before nightfall, he will not be allowed to cross the border. He will have to apply for a new exit permit next morning, when the permit will again be valid for only one day.

Unpleasant as the Albanian reprisals against the Eastern bloc diplomatic agencies may be, they are mild in comparison with the countermeasures taken against Albania in this same period by the Soviet Union and the satellite countries, in the military, diplomatic, and cultural areas. The ambitious program started by the Albanian leaders for the building up of a body of technical intelligentsia among the young people has been seriously imperiled since the summer of 1961. Scientists and lecturers from satellite countries canceled their promised lectures at Albania's only university in Tirana for the winter term 1961–62 at short notice. There can be no doubt about the effect of these cancellations on the young Albanian university, which cannot from its own resources provide the teaching staff necessary for the development of a normal and scientifically based program of instruction. Scientific assistance from the Eastern bloc was desperately needed, and it was inevitable that the Soviet reprisals would lead to a lowering in the quality of training and instruction. In my conversations with them, professors of Tirana University tried to play down the consequences of the Soviet scientific boycott, proudly pointing to the capability of the University's own teaching staff. But however confident they claimed to be, their eyes betrayed their anxiety.

Albania's plans suffered an equally serious setback in the cultural field, when all the Eastern-bloc countries canceled the scholarships on which Albanian students were studying in the Soviet Union and the satellite countries. This blow came completely without warning. The Albanian students had either to return home or, since most of them were on vacation at home when it happened, could not return to the countries where they had been studying. The students on vacation were particularly hard hit by the Soviet measures, since many of them had left their scanty possessions in the university towns where they had been living. Anything they had not actually brought home with them—be it clothing or, more important, study material—they lost. These students not only bewailed the loss of their possessions, they were also worried about their careers and futures, and were quite baffled by this sudden political about-face which seemed to have cut the ground from under their feet.

In my conversations with Albanian students, it was made clear what effects Moscow's order for the cancellation of scholarships will have on Albania's scientific situation, particularly on her technical position. The majority of the Albanians studying in the Eastern-bloc countries had chosen a technical career, which promised a great future. Albania is rich in raw materials, which are not being worked as intensively as they should be because of the lack of technical equipment and the shortage of trained engineers. This was the reason for the large number of Albanian students studying at Eastern-bloc mining and engineering schools. All that has changed. Official statistics issued by the Eastern bloc show a fall in the number of foreign students at these schools. Early in 1962, a Polish statement gave as the reason for this the "discontinuation of studies" by Albanian students this year. But it is less the technical schools in these countries that have to bemoan this loss than the Albanian government, for whom it will mean a great obstacle to the industrialization of their country.

A further reprisal by the Soviets had less far-reaching, although much more impressive consequences for Albania. In the center of Tirana, there stands a gigantic building project. The foundations are in place and the first blocks of concrete have been hauled up. A confusion of pillars, iron frames, and wooden planking gives an idea of the vast proportions the project will one day assume. This is the future "Palace of Culture," a gift from the Soviet Union to Albania. Khrushchev delivered the blueprints for the Palace of Culture to the comrades in Tirana on the occasion of his first visit to Albania early in the summer of 1959. The Kremlin wanted to strengthen the bonds between Tirana and Moscow, not only with fraternal kisses and magnificent demonstrations, but also by means of a present that would go down through the ages as a symbol of the "unbreakable friendship" betwen the two Communist countries. The Palace of Culture was intended to be a kind of matching piece to the colossal Palace of Culture in Warsaw, although the passage of time had meanwhile done away with the excrescences peculiar to Stalinist architecture. In contrast to the Warsaw monstrosity, the Tirana palace would at least not be higher than the government office blocks surrounding it. In depth and width, however, it outdid anything that had ever been built in Tirana before. The old bazaar adjoining Scanderbeg Square in the center of the town, a relic of the days of Turkish rule, had to be almost completely torn down to make room for the new project.

The first spadeful of earth was turned in the spring of 1960, amid universal rejoicing. The speakers on that day vied with each other in their paeans of praise of Moscow and their assurances of undying gratitude. Then the work began. An unbroken stream of equipment and material from the Soviet Union began to arrive in the port of Durazzo. Enormous cranes and gigantic grabs filled the center of Tirana with unaccustomed din.

But within a year the feverish building activity on the site of the future Palace of Culture died away. The Kremlin had abruptly stopped the funds which were to pay for the splendid "gift to the Albanian people." The scaffolding remained deserted, and the cranes stood still in mournful silence. Whenever I walked past the site, the picture was the same. Inside the board fence there was a Sunday atmosphere, with only an occasional laborer to be seen. From somewhere among the chaos and confusion, there would occasionally come a feeble hammering, as if someone was defiantly trying to prove to the Russians that the Albanians could still finish the gigantic project on their own. "We'll carry on building," an indefatigable Albanian functionary told me. But the fact is that the Albanians are quite unable to finish the project in its original form.

Moscow Orders An Economic Boycott

Of all the reprisal measures the Soviets set against the Albanians in the summer of 1961, none hit them harder than the economic boycott. The visitor could hardly fail to notice, even on the first day of his stay in Albania, that an important source of foreign exchange had completely dried up. The empty hotels bore witness to the success of Moscow's efforts to stop all tourist traffic to Albania from the entire Eastern bloc.

Up to this time, the past few years had seen a great increase in the flow of vacationists from the satellite countries to the Adriatic coast resorts. Albania, though small, had a lot to offer: wild, untamed landscapes, the craggy mountains, romantic castles, old fortresses, and sleepy villages. Then there were the people, who still wore their national costume for everyday. There were also the innumerable remains of an ancient past, symbols of the glories of the Greek and Roman eras. And above all there were the wonderful beaches along the Adriatic. Durazzo, with miles of white sands south of the harbor, became a magnet that attracted tourists from all over Communist Europe. A little further south there was the "Albanian Riviera" on the shores of the Ionian Sea, which was becoming increasingly popular. Every travel agency in the Eastern-bloc countries showed alluring posters advertising the delights of a stay in Albania.

On the beach at Durazzo there stood a few villas, built by a handful of rich people before the war, when the beach itself was used almost exclusively by the population of the capital for weekend recreation. After the war, the Party bosses began to take over. They took over the villas built by their capitalist predecessors, and had a few holiday hotels built to accommodate specially deserving

Party comrades. For a long time, the best hotel in Durazzo was reserved for the Ministry of State Security.

Then Tirana became aware of the benefits that an inflow of foreign exchange would bring to the national exchequer. They decided to follow the example of the Soviet and Bulgarian resorts on the Black Sea. Enormous hotels shot up almost overnight, and in the summer months they were filled with shock-brigade workers and functionaries from the various countries of Eastern Europe. Most of them came from East Germany, Poland, Hungary, and Czechoslovakia, but the Russians also discovered the attractions of the jewel of the Adriatic. They made a start in 1960, when 1200 vacationists from all parts of the Soviet Union arrived on the beautiful Albanian coast.

The Soviets seemed to find Albania an attractive place for holidays. During that same year, they opened negotiations with Tirana for extending the tourist traffic from the Soviet Union for years ahead. The result was that the stream of Soviet visitors began to arrive as early as in the first two months of 1961. At this unusual time of the year, the guests in the hotels on the Adriatic were almost all Soviet nationals. More than 500 of them arrived in the first three months of that year. The hotel registers showed that they included engineers and shock-brigade workers from the Ukraine, and visitors from Moscow, Sverdlovsk, the Urals—there was even a group from far-off Magadan, near Russia's Pacific coast.

Then, after the end of April and the beginning of May, 1961, the cyrillic script ceased to appear in the hotel registers. The entries by nationals of the other European Communist states also dried up. During my four weeks in Albania, I did not meet a single tourist from the Soviet Union or the satellite countries. Only on weekends was there anyone to be seen on the beach at Durazzo, and they were staff from the various embassies in Tirana. The hotels on the Adriatic remained deserted. Only a few top Albanian functionaries and artists could afford a holiday in Durazzo.

For this reason I was all the more surprised to meet two groups of visitors from the West. One of them consisted of Italian families, whose men were former partisans who had fought alongside the Albanian Communists against the Germans in World War II.

They were treated particularly well, they traveled around revisiting the sites of old battles, and were regularly visited by senior officers of the Albanian Army and by Party functionaries.

I was even more surprised when one day, in the restaurant of the Adriatic Hotel in Durazzo, I heard the unmistakable sound of American voices from a nearby table. These turned out to belong to a married couple having breakfast while the latest news from the Party newspaper *Zeri I Popullit* was being translated to them. Later on, when the pair had obviously heard that Western journalists were staying in the hotel, they took noticeable pains to avoid any contact with us. It was not until later, when I looked at the register of the hotel in Sarand, on the Albanian Riviera, that I saw that after writing words of praise about Socialist reconstruction and the hope that Albania would continue its glorious progress on the road of Communism, the pair had signed themselves, "An American Workers' Delegation."

The strangeness of visitors from the free world may arouse the interest of the native population, but their number cannot even begin to plug the hole that the cessation of the tourist traffic from the East European countries has made in the Albanian economy. The deserted beaches and empty hotels in all the resorts could not help but depress the spirits of the few visitors. Even the young people seemed to feel it.

The drying-up of the tourist traffic was a bad blow for the Albanians, but it was only one part of the economic measures Moscow took against Albania, and not even the worst. A much heavier blow was the breaking off of all economic cooperation and assistance hitherto provided by the East European Communist states.

Since 1948, the year in which Albania ceased to be a satellite of Yugoslavia and became a satellite of the Soviet Union, the country has been in a state of absolute economic dependence on the Soviets and their European vassals. Everything that has been done and created in this once poor and backward land is entirely due to the assistance it has received from its Communist allies.

The first steps toward the large-scale industrialization of Albania were taken in 1951, when the Communist leaders proclaimed the start of the first Five Year Plan. The main effort was to be devoted to exploiting the country's considerable raw materials, in the form of chrome, copper, nickel, asphalt, oil, and coal. It was expected that at the end of the first Five Year Plan, the proportion of industrial to agricultural production, which was 27.5 to 72.5 per cent in 1950, would be changed to a proportion of 57.5 per cent for industrial and 42.5 per cent for agricultural production. This utopian target was never reached, but the unrealistic figures show where the main weight of the Albanian Communists' efforts lay and, moreover, how much reliance was being placed on support from the Eastern-bloc states. In spite of the fact that the target figures were not nearly attained, the increase in production in certain sectors of heavy industry in the course of the first Five Year Plan was considerable. This was primarily due to the fact that Albanian industry had previously been in such a primitive state that it only required a little effort and a certain amount of concentration on specific economic targets to bring about a very rapid improvement in production.

The economic aid that Albania received during the first Five Year Plan period, especially from the Soviet Union, was not given entirely without ulterior motive. The country's raw materials were undoubtedly most welcome to the Eastern bloc. But no attempt was made to help the Albanians to construct their own refining or processing plants. This was particularly evident in the case of oil. Albania succeeded in raising her crude oil production from 90,000 tons in 1948, to 254,000 tons in 1955, whereas the country's refineries could only handle 30,000 tons, which was not even enough to cover home requirements. In 1952, it was announced that an oil refinery was to be built near Cerrik, with a capacity of 150,000 tons, but this plant was still not ready in 1957. This meant that Albania had to export her crude oil, most of which went to the Soviet Union and Danzig, while Albania herself was forced to import processed oil products from Rumania. The Soviet Union always made up Albania's balance of payments deficit, but this did not alter the fact that the procedures adopted in crude-oil trading with Albania formed an acceptable source of profit for the Soviet Union, but contributed nothing to the development of Albania's industrial capacity.

The year 1956 brought the announcement of the second Five Year Plan, which followed the same general lines as the first one. The main effort was again to be devoted to exploiting Albania's raw materials. Oil production was to be raised by 50 per cent, coal by 49 per cent. The production of the more valuable raw materials was to be increased even more. Agriculture, too, was to receive more attention, and the plan envisaged the collectivization of all agricultural land by 1960, a measure which it was hoped would boost agricultural production by a considerable amount.

Once again the Albanian leaders were confidently relying on support and assistance from the Soviet Union and the satellites. Their hope seemed justified, for there were indications that the Eastern bloc was beginning to pay more attention to Albania's economic needs than they had previously done.

In January, 1949, at the initial meeting of COMECON, the Council for Mutual Economic Assistance, which was composed of the East European economic community, Albania was not even represented. She did not become a member until the following month, but nobody seemed to attach much importance to her entry. Not one of the permanent COMECON committees chose Tirana as its seat. When the various tasks were allocated on a priority basis in 1954, Albania was last on the list. She was told to concentrate on producing chrome and asphalt, and on raising foodstuffs. However, in the following years there were signs of an impending change. COMECON showed itself increasingly interested in Albania's metal ore deposits. A reliable index of Albania's increasing importance in the Eastern-bloc economic community was given by the Eleventh General Assembly, which took place in Tirana in May, 1959. It was regarded as one of the most important decisions taken at this meeting that all members were recommended to step up their assistance to Albania for the purposes of exploiting her raw material reserves.

In the agricultural sphere, too, there was a more intensive program of assistance by the satellite countries, so that by the end of 1959, 85 per cent of Albania's arable land had been collectivized, which meant that collectivization was virtually complete, as the remaining 15 per cent of land lay in areas that were uneconomic anyway. This collectivization, and the mechanization essential to it, could not have been carried out at this rate without the support of the Eastern bloc.

At the Fourth Albanian Party Congress in February, 1961, Enver Hoxha proudly gave an account of what had been accomplished by the second Five Year Plan. More than 250 "economic and cultural projects" had been completed between 1956 and 1961. These included the Karl Marx power plant in the Mahti Valley, the oil refineries at Stalin and Cerrik, a coal mine at Alarup, the copper mine at Kurbneshi, iron and nickel mines in Pishkashi and Cervanaka, and chrome mines in Tropoje and Martanash. Although these extremely costly and complicated installations could never have been completed without financial and technical assistance, at the beginning of 1961 the Albanian leader could only spare a few words to acknowledge the support given to his country by her powerful allies.

In the fall of 1960, Tirana announced the targets of the third Five Year Plan, which were confirmed at the Fourth Party Congress the following February. For the 1961–65 period, even more effort was to be devoted to the country's industrialization; and it was planned that by 1965, the level of industrial production should stand at 51 per cent higher than the 1960 level. A sum of 70.8 billion *lek* was to be invested in expanding the mining of ores, especially copper and nickel ore. Of this amount, 37.1 billion *lek* was to be used for construction work alone.

Ore mining was to be given increased attention in the future also. But there were already signs of a new development in this field. The third Five Year Plan was to include efforts to boost processing and marketing of the raw materials by the Albanians themselves. It can be assumed that preparing for the third Five Year Plan, this new development in Albanian industrial planning was discussed with the Eastern-bloc allies, who undoubtedly promised both financial and technical assistance. On announcing the setting up, between 1961 and 1965, of a huge project for the processing of chrome and nickel, Hoxha said that the Soviet Union and Czechoslovakia would make a considerable contribution to the construction of this industrial center at Miloti, north of Tirana.

In his speech at the same Party Congress, Mehmet Shehu confirmed that Albania's Communist allies had agreed among themselves to help with the reshaping of Albania's industry. The start of the third Five Year Plan would see the initiation of the country's own processing industries. As examples, Shehu mentioned the construction of several plants for the processing of chrome and other high-quality ores, the building "with Soviet assistance" of a fertilizer plant in Fier, a chemical plant in Lac, "which we shall be asking the Czechs to help us with," a new coal mine near Tirana, an iron and nickel mine in Prenjas, another coal mine, two saw mills, a cement plant, "and a number of other factories to be built with the help of the Soviet Union."

In February, 1961, the Albanian leaders were still firmly relying on large-scale aid from the East European Communist countries. Long before the third Five Year Plan targets had been made public, agreements covering economic and financial assistance to Albania by her allies had been concluded—agreements which assured the attainment of the Plan's targets.

As far back as 1958, it had been announced that the Soviet Union would provide $83.75 million for Albania's "industrial development," of which $75 million would be allocated for "important projects in the course of the third Five Year Plan." The other $8.75 million was intended to be used in expanding the production of oil. In the same year, Czechoslovakia had guaranteed Albania $25 million for the development of "the mining and transporting of nickel ore," and East Germany furnished $10 million "for various requirements and industrial installations." Poland, too, offered financial aid "for miscellaneous industrial equipment," although the amount was not specified. Then, in January, 1959, Red China added her offering to the collective assistance being provided for Albania's economic development, giving Tirana the comparatively modest sum of $13.75 million for "the purchase of equipment for industrial projects during the period of 1961–65."

Even before the public announcement of the third Five Year Plan, therefore, the Communist states had already promised Albania $132.5 million, plus a small Polish contribution. Considering Albania's comparatively meager industrial potential, this sum was considerable. It certainly created favorable preconditions for the realization of the Plan itself.

Since the fall of 1960, however, the Soviet and satellite press has ceased to carry stories about promises of financial assistance to Albania. At first, the men in the Kremlin did not seem to be absolutely certain whether the growing political and ideological tension ought to be allowed to affect the economic situation. The last word had still not been spoken, and in the first weeks of 1961, Moscow was still trying to stave off an ugly situation by offering to extend Soviet trade agreements with Tirana.

Figures published in 1958 show that more than half of Albania's total foreign trade was with the Soviet Union. Albanian imports from Russia alone amounted to 2.25 million *lek*. The agreement envisaged an increase of 7 per cent in Soviet-Albanian trade. To come even within sight of fulfilling her trade obligations, Albania had to bring about a sizable increase in her exports to the Eastern-bloc countries. This, in turn, depended on an expansion of her heavy industries, particularly on the modernization and expansion of her mining industry. The result was that Albania's ability to export was directly linked to the economic and financial assistance promised by the Soviet Union and her satellites. With the offer to extend the trade agreements, the Eastern bloc was giving Albania stern warning of the seriousness of her position. But Tirana refused to heed the warning.

The Kremlin's patience was now exhausted. With one blow, the Soviets and their satellites canceled their economic aid and revoked their promises of financial credit. Moscow dispatched an ultimatum demanding the repayment of loans already made, although these were not to have been repayable until 1970. In April and May, 1961, all Soviet specialists working in Albania were recalled. The other Communist countries set August 31 as the deadline by which all their technicians and engineers were to leave.

All this put Albania in a precarious situation. Not only was the third Five Year Plan now most unlikely to be realized, but the general economic boycott by the Communist countries also meant that current supplies and provisions for the Albanian people themselves were seriously imperiled. Moscow's cultural reprisals threatened to ruin the Albanian government's training and education schemes, and the military countermeasures had demonstrated beyond doubt how weak Albania's isolated position was without the promise of assistance by her allies. The Tirana regime might well find itself having to cope with the domestic effects of the situation.

In this difficult hour, a new offer of help arrived. It was not entirely unexpected, but the Albanians had not been sure they could reckon with it in all circumstances. Peking stretched out a hand to its political and ideological supporters, and in doing so deliberately and publicly crossed Moscow's plans.

Big Brother Comes to the Rescue

The Chinese were the most cheerful people I met anywhere in Albania. Always smiling and full of fun, they seemed to feel perfectly happy on outpost duty in the Mediterranean. Nonetheless, they were both hard working and disciplined. Although they had adapted themselves to wear Western-style clothing, rather than the notorious blue uniform clothes that give their homeland such an unpleasantly militant appearance, there was still a gulf between them and the people around them. In Durazzo, I had a good opportunity to take a long look at the Chinese visitors. I saw that, while they were always polite, they still kept entirely to themselves. It was difficult, if not impossible, to get into conversation with them, not only for the few foreigners living in the hotel, but even for the Albanians.

Every morning, on the stroke of eight, jeeps and buses picked them up from the hotel and took them nobody knew where. Each evening they reappeared, to have a swim or to play about like children on the beach. At a given time, they disappeared as if on a signal: It was time to start the political indoctrination lesson. The sing-song voices of the instructors would be heard from the part of the hotel where the Chinese lived, and then there would be the sounds of animated discussion.

They had free time, too, but they used it much more intensively than any of the other guests, sitting in the hotel foyer reading or studying the Albanian language, or poring over thick technical volumes. Occasionally, a group would get together for communal singing, and the strange sounds that floated through the hotel only emphasized the strange, almost eerie situation that had come about as a result of the Albanian leaders' change of political course.

One day I found a young Chinese sitting on the hotel terrace, practicing on some kind of Chinese stringed instrument. This seemed a good opportunity to try to get into conversation with him. What could be more harmless than a talk about music? I decided that as soon as the musician paused for a moment, I would open my remarks in Russian, assuming that I would be more likely to get a favorable reaction with a "socialist" than with a "capitalist" language. But his reaction, when I cautiously tried to begin a conversation about Chinese music, was not only abrupt but downright boorish. He sprang to his feet, turned on his heel, and was gone without even a glance in my direction—as though I had uttered some mortal insult. I could only think that news of my country of origin and my profession had got around the hotel; or perhaps it was the sounds of Russian that had this effect on him.

There seems to be no way of finding out how many Chinese technicians and specialists have arrived in Albania. There are no official figures on this. But dozens of them are to be seen in Durazzo and even more in Tirana, where they are quartered in one large wing of the Dajti Hotel. In general, when they enter the hotel it is only to sleep. An East German engineer told me in derisive tones that the Chinese could not afford to eat in the Dajti, and congregated in the cheaper and more popular *Domica*. This is not surprising. The Chinese technicians are paid much less than their predecessors from the Soviet Union and the satellite countries. A fitter from East Germany told me he made 16,000 *lek* a month, while his successor, the Chinese fitter, only received 8,000.

The Relieving Force From China

While it does not look as though the cultural and military aid provided by the Chinese has reached any significant proportion as yet, in the economic sector the Chinese have taken over a large part of the role previously played by the East European Communist bloc. An economic agreement between Tirana and Peking was concluded in April, 1961, following a visit to Peking by a delegation of ranking Albanian functionaries, headed by Abdyl Kellezi. Negotiations had actually begun in February, but it appears that the agreement was reached only after the Fourth Albanian Party Congress, when Moscow's measures put Albania in a desperate position. China pledged herself to invest $123 million in the third Five Year Plan, the funds to be used for the purchase of machines and other equipment for "twenty-five large industrial plants." The implication of this was that China had now become the mainstay of the Albanian industrialization program, since the Chinese had assumed almost the same amount of obligations in credits and financial aid as Albania had previously been promised by the Soviet Union and the satellites. And there were signs that China was prepared to go even beyond that figure.

As in the case of the purely financial aid, China also filled the gap left by the withdrawal of technical assistance by the Soviet Union and the satellites. While East European specialists and technicians were leaving Albania or getting ready to do so, Chinese technicians came streaming in. Engineers from the Far East took over the supervision of Albanian mining undertakings and helped in the planning of new industrial projects.

Relations between the East Europeans and the newly arrived Chinese were anything but harmonious, and this was paralleled by the tension that had begun to build up between the Albanians and the experts from the Eastern-bloc states. An engineer from East Germany told me of the difficulties he and his companions had encountered. They had spent some years in the copper-processing plant in Kurbneshi in Northern Albania. It had not been easy to accustom the Albanian hands, who had no feeling for exacting technical work, to order and discipline. There had been continued friction. However, this was a problem that had to be faced not only by the Germans, the Czechs, and the Russians, but also by the Albanian leaders themselves. It is no simple matter to make qualified technical workers out of people who, until only a short while before, had led a free and untrammeled existence as shepherds in the mountains.

Whereas relations between the East European specialists and

their Albanian subordinates were already strained, they became strained almost to breaking point with the first signs of the political change of course. The Albanians, recognizing their own weaknesses and their helplessness, became irritable; they tried to cover up their feeling of uncertainty by all kinds of sharp practice and malevolence. Albanians who were skilled workers had very mixed feelings about the impending departure of their European advisers and the arrival of the Chinese experts, and they also found it necessary to cover up their ebbing confidence. In the course of everyday business, the Albanians lost no chance of letting the European specialists know they regarded them as traitors to the common cause. The Albanian functionaries became fractious, refused to listen to any advice, and made cooperation painful and unpleasant. In private life, vexations and petty meannesses were practiced on the families of the technicians. In short, what had been pioneering work in a new land gradually turned into a life of misery.

The political leaders also took every opportunity to visit their anger at the Moscow-inspired reprisals on the East European specialists. For example, a number of East German technicians turned up in Tirana for the 1961 May Day celebrations, for which they had previously been treated as prominent guests at the parades and demonstrations. The main boulevard, "New Albania Boulevard," had been decorated, and the dais for the Party and governmental leaders and foreign missions had been set up in front of the Dajti Hotel. Hitherto, it had been the practice to give the leading personalities among the East European experts seats on the dais among the guests of honor. This year, however, the East European engineers were instructed by the Albanian security authorities not to appear. They were forced to stay in their hotel rooms, so they got ready to watch the show from their hotel-room windows. When the parade began and the first columns were approaching the saluting base, accompanied by cheers and the sound of martial music, security men suddenly appeared in the hotel rooms and ordered the technicians to close the windows and not to leave their rooms. The security men then let down the blinds on the windows, so that the technicians saw nothing and had to be content to vent their anger in curses, while outside "the fraternal solidarity of the Socialist camp" was being celebrated with wild enthusiasm.

In the spring and summer of 1961, the East German legation in Tirana gave the technicians under its charge a series of instructions on how they should conduct themselves in this new situation. One circular, for example, warned them that since April, all mail home had been censored by the Albanians. The specialists were therefore advised not to say anything detrimental to Albania and the Albanians, and particularly to avoid saying anything that might give a hint of the increasing difficulties of everyday life, and the tension between Albania and East Germany. "Don't make any trouble" was the general tenor of the instructions.

This kind of action at the lower level managed to ensure the avoidance of conflicts and of annoying intervention by the Albanians. At the top level, however, there was no way of avoiding the effects of the existing situation. There was no longer any sign of "Socialist solidarity," as I learned from one of the German engineers from the copper-processing plant at Kurbneshi. The East German authorities had instructed the German technicians employed at this plant to be out of Albania by August 31, even though this put them in breach of contract. As soon as the Albanian Government learned of this, they set every possible wheel in motion to try to prevent or at least put off the departure of the German experts. Representatives of the Albanian planning departments traveled to Pankow, the seat of the East German Government, and asked for the departure date to be changed, their main argument being that the Chinese reliefs would not be arriving until January, 1962. But the East German functionaries refused to budge, and by August 31, all the German technicians had left Kurbneshi, leaving the Albanians without qualified supervising staff.

The copper plant at Kurbneshi is a modern, highly technical project. German engineers not only built it up, but the direction of the production process had been completely in their hands ever since the plant started, in May, 1960. Eleven Albanian engineers had been sent to East Germany for training, but German experts assured me that it is doubtful whether that will be sufficient. For one thing, only a few of the Albanian technicians who had been trained in modern techniques in East Germany still carried out the correct procedures on their return to their homeland. Most of them quickly reverted to the slap-happy attitudes customary in Albania. The Germans who left were certain that a few months under Albanian direction would suffice to ruin the plant.

Another example of "socialist solidarity" was given to me by a Czech engineer. The mining of nickel in Albania had always been the province of Czech experts, and it was Czechoslovakia that provided the greatest amount of technical and financial aid for the production of nickel in Central Albania. The Albanians were supposed to repay the loans, machinery, and equipment by exporting raw nickel ore to Czechoslovakia, where the processing was to be done. For this purpose, the Czechs began to construct a nickel-processing plant in Slovakia in 1959. However, differences arose between Albania and Czechoslovakia. Albania, it was claimed, was not keeping its part of the agreement. In an effort to make extra profit, Albania was selling the ore to other countries. She was particularly interested in getting Italy as a customer, for the sake of the much-needed hard currency. This annoyed the Czechs, who not only upbraided the Albanians, but also filed suit against them—although in the interests of "solidarity," the "trials" were never allowed to come to anything. In 1960, things took a different direction when a Chinese delegation suggested that the Albanians would do much better to run the profitable nickel-processing themselves. The Chinese even promised to provide all the assistance the Albanians might need, and the Albanians accepted. Today, a new industrial project is under construction in Pishkashki, in Central Albania, where the modern plant will deal with nickel in all its stages, from the mining to the refining, under Chinese supervision. The Czechs will be left with the Slovakian processing plant on their hands.

Everywhere I went, I saw the same picture: The European specialists were moving out, and Chinese were taking their places. The course of events I described in regard to the copper and nickel industry is happening in other sectors also. The harbor at Durazzo, for example, which had always been too small to cope with the amount of marine traffic coming in, was to have been extended and rebuilt with the help of East German construction experts. These plans were dropped on the change of political climate, and since the early summer of 1961, it is the Chinese who have taken over the tasks the East Germans were to have carried out in the harbor. The same thing happened in the case of the plans to build a cold-storage plant in the port of Durazzo. This project was also to have been supervised by East German specialists, but it never got any further than the planning stage.

Belgrade–Moscow–Peking

By the middle of 1961, with the willing consent of the Albanian leaders, the Chinese had succeeded in establishing a bridgehead in Europe. This was the second time the Albanians had chosen to alter course, changing their economic partners and most important financial patrons. The rejection of the support previously offered by the mighty Soviet partner and the change to the Chinese colossus, the strength of whose position is still in doubt, is an experiment that seems fraught with danger. The perils are so obvious and the advantages so problematical that one wonders how Albania could have brought itself to take such a risky step. The history of previous changes of heart gives some idea of the nature of recent events and the motives underlying them.

After 1944, the year in which the independence of a Communist Albania had been proclaimed, it was Yugoslavia who provided a considerable amount of sustenance for the young state. Albania had enough economic potential. It was now only a matter of exploiting that potential, and Yugoslavia showed herself eager to help in this. The economic planning of both countries was coordinated, a customs union created, their currencies were aligned with each other, and a series of undertakings of interest to both sides was set in motion. For example, both countries worked together on a new railroad project. Hundreds of Yugoslav economic experts streamed into Albania.

Albania became a satellite of Yugoslavia, just as Yugoslavia in turn was a satellite of the Soviet Union. The Albanian leaders were aware of the possible consequences of this situation, and they kept a sharp eye on it. The economic fusion of the two countries was well advanced, and the Albanian leaders knew that if they did not take care, they would find their country gradually being reduced to the status of a dependency of Yugoslavia.

Nobody saw this possibility more clearly than Stalin. In his biography of Tito, Vladimir Dedijer tells how Stalin, not long before the outbreak of the Cominform conflict, was in conversation with Milovan Djilas, in those days still an intimate confidant of Tito. On the Yugoslav question, Stalin said, "The Soviet government makes no claims of any kind on Albania. It is open to Yugoslavia to swallow Albania whenever she wants to." Djilas was astonished at this remark and replied that the question was not one of "swallowing" Albania, but of friendly relations between two countries. "Oh well," interjected Molotov, "that comes to the same thing."

Opinions may vary as to the truth of this story, but it does illustrate Albania's position of dependence on Yugoslavia in those days. It goes without saying that Yugoslavia was not prompted by unselfish motives, as the Yugoslavians would have you believe. True, they did provide Albania with food, weapons, and equipment of all kinds after World War II. The total value—calculated at an artificial rate of exchange—was said to have been in the region of $80 million. Nevertheless, Belgrade also had its own interests at heart. The whole of the Albanian export trade was handled by a central agency in Belgrade. The Yugoslavs established a series of so-called "joint Albanian-Yugoslav associations" in Albania, following the pattern that the Soviets had introduced into Yugoslavia and the other satellites. When Belgrade broke with Moscow, the Yugoslavs called these associations "a means of imperialist penetration."

Still, Yugoslav assistance to Albania in those first difficult years must not be underrated. Yugoslavia's contribution to Albania's finance took care of 57 per cent of the budget, and in 1948, it still took care of 50 per cent. Shortly after 1948, Tito broke with the Kremlin. The Albanians saw their chance and went over to Moscow's side, thus freeing themselves of their subordination to Yugoslavia. From then on, the Soviets assumed the burden of building up the Albanian economy, and their satellites were instructed to act likewise.

Figures on the extent of the Soviet Union's assistance to Albania have never been published, but it is known to have been considerable. In 1957, the Soviets canceled an Albanian debt to them of more than $40 million. Analysis of the trade agreements in force at this time shows that 90 per cent of the technical equipment for Albania's oil industry alone was provided by the Soviet Union. Sixty-five per cent of the agricultural machinery, and 82 per cent of Albania's stock of tractors also came from the Soviet Union.

In February, 1961, Albania made its second shift of allegiance. From now on, it was the Chinese who were to provide the necessary financial resources. Nevertheless, the proportion of home to foreign capital investment remained about the same. Roughly speaking, about one half of Albania's financial requirements are always provided by the ally of the moment. This was certainly true at the time of Albania's dependence on Yugoslavia, and was probably little different during the years of her connection with Moscow.

Conversations I had with Albanians left me with the impression that responsible functionaries are not entirely happy about the prospects of future collaboration with their new partners. There is some doubt about the genuineness of China's ability to live up to her financial promises, and there is doubt about the quality of the Chinese specialists now streaming into the country. There is concern about the change from the familiar and well-tried methods to new ones, and about how collaboration with a little-known partner from thousands of miles away will work out. And Albania is afraid of the possibility that the Communist boycott measures may be extended to trade as well. There were some signs of this in the summer of 1961; and even the trade treaties the Soviet Union and some satellite countries signed at the beginning of 1961, which envisaged an increase in the volume of trade, cannot hide these signs. Albania is in a very difficult position, having had an adverse trade balance with the most important of her Eastern-bloc trading partners for years. If the Eastern-bloc countries were to decide to restrict their exports to Albania to the volume of Albania's exports to them, the planners in Tirana would really be in a desperate situation. Imports would then have to be very greatly reduced, for it is highly unlikely that the Chinese would be able to make up the deficiency in foodstuffs and consumer goods.

For these reasons, the change of allies was accompanied by the introduction of measures reflecting the apprehension of the Albanian leaders. In the fall of 1961, the Central Committee of the Albanian Communist Party announced the passing of a resolution aimed at a "policy of intensive economy" and a "mobilization of domestic reserves." A law was also passed decreeing that from October 1, 1961, all Albanians had to work a ten-hour day twice a week. The Albanian leaders are well aware of the sacrifices that their country's third economic metamorphosis will entail, and make no secret of their feeling that Albania is faced with what may be painful times.

Albania has often been called "the test-tube Communist satellite." There is hardly any other Communist state in which the ebb and flow of basic political and ideological differences within the Communist bloc can be so clearly observed. What is more, in accepting the risks to their country entailed by a revolt against Moscow, the country's leaders have reaffirmed their belief in the validity of the principle—binding on all Communist states—that the requirements of the general political line must take priority over any purely economic ties. Only an analysis of these political and ideological motives can make clear how the sensational events in Moscow could ever have come about.

III

The Factors Behind the Revolt

IN NO OTHER Iron Curtain country is there so extensive a police and surveillance machine as in Albania. The *Sigurimi*, as the secret police is called, are everywhere that people assemble. Foreigners are still kept under strict surveillance, but the enormous machine is not there merely to keep an eye on the foreigners. It covers the Albanians as well, in the university classrooms, on ships, trains, and street cars. No foreigner can move without his permanent escort, and no foreigner can hope to exchange more than a few words with a native Albanian before the *Sigurimi* appear, and the Albanian scuttles away in panic.

Fear is written on the faces of the people, especially those who have managed to climb a rung or two on the social ladder. Nobody dares to risk degradation and disgrace. Nobody knows for certain how many people have already been sacrificed to the totalitarian Moloch, but a United Nations report put the figure of political arrests between 1945 and 1956 at 80,000, of whom 16,000 have perished in jails or concentration camps. This is a terrifying figure in view of the smallness of the total population, and the actual number of people the Communists might feel could be dangerous to them. Nobody knows for certain what has happened in Albania since 1956.

In 1961, one of the men I spoke to told me that it was only recently that the wave of arrests had died down somewhat. But this does not tell us much about the extent of the terror still ruling in Albania. The events of past years have scared the Albanians into submissiveness, and submissiveness in the people increases the security of the state. Furthermore, arrests can be increased whenever the situation demands it. At the beginning of 1960, the government issued a decree by which any Albanian citizen can be interned and outlawed without due process of law, merely by administrative action. Even in this tiny country, there are still said to be fourteen concentration camps where political prisoners are detained.

Just as in the Soviet Union in the dark days of Stalin's rule, the Albanian Communist Party holds its subjects in its iron grip by means of a merciless police. The people most affected are those in the Party machine itself, followed by the intellectuals, who have suffered severely. A particularly persecuted group, however, has been the religious community.

All over the country, both churches and mosques are falling into decay. The contributions by the faithful poor and the meager funds provided by the state are not sufficient to save the buildings from the ravages of time and weather. The church in Sarand stands in the form of a shaky wooden building with a bell, rescued from former times, on a rickety frame. In Scutari, the slender tower of the Franciscan monastery still rises above the town, but within the walls are the unmistakable signs of dilapidation. The faces of Albania's last remaining seven monks are full of despair, helplessness, and resignation. Neither organ nor choir can testify to the proud assurance of the Catholic community that once made Scutari one of the rising cultural centers of Albania. No one knows how long even this symbol of religious life will be able to stand in the face of the hurricane of atheistic propaganda.

The fate of the Orthodox church on the hill at the southern edge of Tirana is plain for all to see. It has been converted into a restaurant. The altar has been turned into a counter, on which a chromium-plated coffee machine is displayed as the latest "socialist achievement." Where the ikons once stood are batteries of bottles of cheap Albanian liquor. The nave is full of tables, at which the new class consumes its *kebab* and *shashlik* to the wailing sounds of popular songs.

The time is long past when the Albanian Communist regime displayed tolerance and even goodwill toward the religious communities. In those days, when Moscow's appointed governors were not yet certain of their power, and a pretense of genuinely democratic demeanor had to be made both to the peoples of the Communist countries and to the Western world, Enver Hoxha and his minions attended services held by the three most important confessions in order to give their "thanks" for the country's "liberation." But that attitude soon changed. Confessional schools were closed, the religious press forbidden, and all church property sequestrated. The religious communities had to accept financial dependence on the state, even if only to be able to pay their priests and to continue some sort of church life. The atheistic propaganda put out by the Communists was not without its effect, especially on young people. However, it took the cruel and brutal persecution of the churches and their leaders to produce the condition of paralysis and resignation that characterizes religious life in Albania today.

The oppressors struck at all the faiths even if the degree of oppression varied. The strongest, Moslemism, which embraces 60-70 per cent of the people, was crippled by the arrests of all Mohammedan dignitaries who appeared likely to be able to resist the Communist dictators. Of the total of 530 mosques which used to function in Albania, only a few dozen are still active. All contacts with the spiritual centers in the East, and especially with the Al-Azhar University in Cairo, have been cut off. The different sects were played off one against the other. Even the most fanatical group, the Bektashi, who transfered their center from Ankara to Tirana after Kemal's revolution in 1922, has been smashed. It is rare today to see any of the faithful acknowledging their faith by public prayer. Albanian Islam is in its death throes.

The treatment accorded the members of the Albanian Orthodox Church, to which about 20 per cent of the people belong, was slightly better. After the war, they tried to maintain their centuries-old independence. But in the end, they were subjected to the same measures of oppression as the members of other faiths. Two bishops were arrested and the primate was deposed, his place being taken by a priest loyal to Communism. Shortly after this, the one-time independent church made known its submission to the Moscow patriarchate, which meant that henceforth it would be liable to any kind of political manipulation.

The church least liable to molestation in present-day Albania is the Greek Orthodox Church.

The main weight of terrorist tactics has been laid on the small but valiant Roman Catholic community. Although only 10 per

cent of the people belonged to it, the Communist regime seems to
have regarded it as especially dangerous for two reasons: First,
the Catholic clergy were the most assiduous in trying to lead the
people out of illiteracy, and had established flourishing cultural
centers; and second, the Catholics, particularly those in the
northern mountain country, had always been ready to resort to
arms to defend such concepts as honor, freedom, and independence. They were inimical to the Communists.

The Communists were primarily out to break up the Catholics'
international connections. With calculated cruelty, they set to
work to destroy the hierarchy. Of the two archbishops and four
bishops, not one is still in office. Two were shot after staged
"trials," and one died in prison. According to available reports, 17
out of 93 priests were shot, and 39 are in jail. Of 94 monks, 16
were shot, 35 sent to jail or to concentration camps, and 31 de-
ported. In 1951, a schismatic National Catholic Church of Albania
was founded, its statutes precluding any connection with Rome.
Since then, there has been no correspondence with Rome, even
on matters of pure dogma. No new bishops can be appointed.
There are no theological colleges, and the few who do study for
orders cannot be consecrated. But despite the merciless persecution, there are still the faithful who remain true to their church.
They fill the Franciscan Church in Scutari on Sundays, just as, I
was told, they stream into the village churches up in the mountains.

The situation of the church in Albania seems to be hopeless.

Who Benefits from the Regime?

The reign of terror and malevolence employed against all potential opponents serve the purposes of the Party. But the Party is
nothing more than the small clique that Enver Hoxha has gathered
around himself. It has often been maintained in the West that the
top men in Communist Albania consist mainly of members of a
class of intellectuals from tribal and family groups. The Albanians
are divided into two main branches, the Geghs in the north and
the Tosks in the south. Of the two, it was the southern Tosks who
played the decisive role in the development of the Albanian

Communist Party, whose existence was conditioned mainly by prewar social conditions and the course of the struggle carried on by the partisans during the war. Until the Communists came to power, the northern Geghs lived mostly in tightly knit tribal units, whereas the Tosks were held together by the much looser connection that, say, feudal serfs would have with the landed gentry. This latter connection fostered the growth of an agricultural proletariat, and the formation of a very shallow intellectual stratum.

The effects of the social differences between the two main branches in Albania made themselves particularly evident during World War II. In his book *Sons of the Eagle,* Julian Amery, the British Liaison Officer to the Gegh nationalist resistance forces, relates how the southern Communist partisans, made up of troops of agricultural workers and led by intellectually trained leaders, cleverly outmaneuvered the northern resistance forces from the tribal areas, and finally came out on top. This development was helped along, it must be admitted, by the naive policies of the Allied Headquarters in Bari. Another characteristic that marked the Albanian leaders for a number of years was the extent to which they were interrelated either by blood or by marriage. In early 1961, the Yugoslav newspaper *Borba* published a table showing that the Central Committee of the Albanian Communist Party contained five married couples and that twelve of the other members were blood relations. (However, it must be remembered that Yugoslav statements and analyses of this kind in regard to Albania are not always very objective.) The reason for the family connections within the council of Communist leaders is easily understood. During the build-up of the top ranks of the Communist movement after the war there were not many intellectually and ideologically qualified candidates to choose from. Moreover, the years of bitter partisan fighting had welded the leading personalities together—the community of experience in the barren mountain areas created relationships that extended far beyond the purely political.

However, too much importance should not be attached to the differences between Geghs and Tosks. Differences there are, of course, as was openly confirmed not only by people in Scutari, but also in the south, where I heard occasional joking remarks about the northern Geghs. Yet for all that, I was also told that the rivalry between the two main groups is dying out. Both sides consider themselves members of one nation, sitting in the same boat, and experiencing the same fate. The enemies of Albania are felt to be the enemies of both groups. This is true on the Party political level as well. One of the top-ranking men, Lt.-General Bequir Balluku, the Defense Minister who has been a member of the Politbureau for years, is a Gegh. Another Gegh is Ramiz Alia, who was given a seat in the Politbureau and taken into the Central Committee at the Fourth Party Congress in February, 1961. Alia's career can be taken as symptomatic of the decline in enmity between the Geghs and the Tosks.

Even though tribal and family relationships play a less important part in the group that controls Albania's affairs, the fact remains that Enver Hoxha regards an elite group as the mainstay of his power and the country's security. The clan exercises unfettered power and unconcernedly enjoys its privileges. There is not much evidence of bonds of "solidarity with the toiling masses." Members of the clan lead their own lives, sealed off from the mass of the people.

I was continually surprised that the openly practiced class privilege seemed to be so little resented by the ordinary man-in-the-street. Perhaps this unconcern is rooted in the fact that class differences have always existed in Albania. Basically, then, the Communists are only carrying on what has been the normal way of life since anyone can remember. Nevertheless, the glaring contrast between proletarian theory and proletarian practice must have made the top men uncomfortable, for in 1958, they adopted an experiment that was started by the Chinese: Manual labor was decreed for the intellectual and administrative elite. Every functionary and official would be required to spend one month a year doing physical work. Some spend their month by working as gardeners in the Tirana public gardens, some carry around books and files in libraries or ministries, and others work on the collective farms in their home villages.

This experiment was in line with the Party pronouncement that the higher ranks must not lose touch with the masses. However, this "solidarity" with the toilers did not extent to paying the functionaries, during their compulsory labor period, the same wages as the workers.

It is not class privilege, however, but the permanent reign of terror and the pitiless despotism that seem to me to be the main reasons for a smoldering, and as yet hardly definable, dissatisfaction all over Albania. The signs of this dissatisfaction used to be the repeated "purges." Now there is a new source of uneasiness—cynicism toward the Party's new pro-Chinese line. The change of direction was not brought about without dissension within the Party itself.

Belishova and Tashko have disappeared from sight, and their names are dirty words. Nobody knows what became of them. Since their disappearance, the Party cadres have been still. Nobody seems to feel himself big enough to take on Enver Hoxha. Nobody mentions the "treason trial" or the arrest of the two Foreign Ministry officials if he can avoid it, for there is only too obvious a connection between these and the complex and delicate background to the Albanian switch of loyalties. Nobody cares to say a single word he might later have cause to regret.

All the same, the people still display a lively interest in political events. They are not very much interested in the details of foreign policy, nor are they able to comprehend the quasi-hierological conflict of ideas that takes place in the councils of the leaders of international Communism. They feel that there has been a development that may affect them personally far more directly than the abstract wrangles between the leaders. It is common knowledge that Albania's position is getting worse. The economic boycott is making itself felt. The Party has quietly let it be known that anyone who can afford to do so should lay in a stock of goods, for there are difficult times ahead. The people are not blind to the consequences of the new development, and there is a growing feeling of uneasiness among them.

Shortly before I left Albania, a man with an intimate knowledge of the domestic climate told me that Enver Hoxha had never before been in so dangerous a position. This opinion was based on his belief that the disquiet felt by the people must lead to fresh dissension within the Party. He also felt that past experience entitled one to believe that some of the Communist "brother parties" would not stand idly by, and that they would put every possible obstacle in the way of Albania's new pro-Chinese policy.

This ominous prophecy, even from an expert in these matters, cannot be taken completely at face value. In the past, Hoxha has often enough demonstrated his determination to beat down all opposition at whatever cost. And there can be little doubt about the way the men around Hoxha will react if the people's anxiety should increase and centers of resistance should be formed. Despotic and severe repressive measures have proved efficacious in dealing with critical situations, ever since the Communists came to power in Albania. Hoxha and his minions are firm believers in the maxims of Joseph Stalin. The old Bolshevik rule that every available means must be used to break opposition to the regime if that opposition endangers the existence of the "workers' and peasants' state" also holds good in Albania.

The question that arises in the observer's mind, however, is this: Why did the Albanian leaders let matters go so far? Again, why is it that in contrast to developments in most of the other European Communist countries, the "sword of the proletariat," the State Security Police, is still the real and dominating instrument of power in Albania? Why do the Albanian Communists still adhere to Stalinist principles and refuse to follow the general line accepted—even if in varying degree—by all the Eastern-bloc states since the 1956 Twentieth Party Congress in Moscow?

"Stalin For Ever!"

These were the questions I put to an Albanian functionary. "Come back to Albania in six years' time, and you will find that there will have been great changes," was his reply. He meant that by then the universal oppression and the shackles on intellectual freedom would have given way to a more "liberal" atmosphere. As things were, the regime could not afford to allow any relaxation of the restrictions they had imposed. Any attempt to "let a hundred flowers bloom" in Albania would lead to chaos far worse than the Chinese Party had experienced and would open the door to "revisionism and imperialism."

When they took over the government of Albania, the Communists found that the conditions in which they had to make their first beginnings bore no resemblance to those in the highly industrialized Communist countries of Central Europe. They had to start at the bottom. The country was very backward, and there was no industry to speak of. The raw materials first had to be found, and methods of mining had to be discovered. The majority of the population was illiterate, born and bred in an atmosphere of tradition and custom more appropriate to the Middle Ages than to the twentieth century. Religious superstition was universal. Moreover, the Communist leaders knew that the people they had to deal with were not apathetic, adaptable, or patient men and women, but extremely self-willed, individualistic and aggressive ones, who had their own ideas about their rights. It was clear from the outset that the introduction of modern, progressive ideas, of socialism—and later of Communism—was not going to be possible on the basis of persuasion or instruction. Against the kind of stubborn resistance that was innate in the people's traditional way of life and thought, only one method would bring results—drastic severity. The Albanian leaders did employ that method, exactly as was done in the other newly established Communist countries of Eastern Europe.

From the point of view of the Albanian Communists, therefore, the question was not whether the use of the mailed fist in the enforcement of socialism was desirable or not, but simply whether or not it was necessary in the present phase of development. As things stood, they argued, the Government still could not afford to cover the mailed fist with the velvet glove. Expressed in Communist jargon, "the awareness of the people had not been sufficiently reorganized." The socialist way of life was not as yet firmly rooted. There were still currents of resistance at various levels, the existence of which justified the imposition of drastic measures to protect what had been attained so far. Only the ruthless use of force, the Government felt, would ensure the continued rise of Communism, making it possible one day to relax the iron grip.

Having put forth this argument, the Albanian Communists also put forth its corollary: If this line of thinking is correct, they said, then the charges made against Tirana by the East European Communist leaders are unwarranted. As for the accusation of "Stalinism," what did this really mean when all is said and done? There was a time when those very East European countries not only revered Stalin as a demigod, a genius in every department of life, but paid him homage and adoration, such as had seldom been accorded to any man. As far as the Soviet Union was concerned, it was there above all that Stalin was regarded as the great exemplar. It was Stalin who made Soviet Russia what she is today. But who can deny that in so doing Stalin was forced to use methods that the Albanian Communists would rather not be using today? Unfortunately, the one was inseparable from the other. If you wanted the "greatest revolution in the history of mankind," then you had to accept the cost of bringing it about. Robespierre said it, Lenin took the same view, Stalin acted in accordance with it, and all that Hoxha now did was to follow their example. The present-day leaders of the Soviet Union could not deny the effectiveness of Stalin's policies in their country. They wanted to forget the consequences of those policies, but the fact was that they could not be forgotten, so that the so-called "destalinization" was pure hypocrisy. The Albanian Communist Government, they maintained, simply could not afford a soft and humane regime in the present stage of Albanian development, any more than the Soviet Union could afford it when she was in a similar stage.

The conclusion the Albanian Communists drew from all this was that their fellow-Communists in the other countries were simply being dishonest, both to themselves and to the Albanians. It was perfectly possible that the leaders of the Soviet Communist Party felt the time had come when they could adopt milder methods in realizing their aims. But the Soviet Union, as the Albanians fully admitted, was much further developed than Albania. The Albanians believed, too, that the Soviet Communists were entitled to the preeminent position within the Eastern bloc. They had reached a position in all spheres of life that Albania was nowhere near attaining. Nobody in Tirana would claim to be able to assess the Soviet Union's internal situation; that was purely a matter for the Soviet comrades. In the same way, it was presumptuous on the part of the Soviet leaders to believe they could correctly assess the situation in Albania; nor were they entitled to lay down the methods the Albanians should employ in any given phase of development.

This general line of argument, which I heard repeatedly from Albanian Communists, always led up to the final tenet that Stalin is and will remain the model for the Albanian Party.

No doubt the arguments stated above have a certain inner logic of their own. But I could never feel quite satisfied, and I repeatedly stated my objections to them. It is undeniable, I would say, that Albania is at a lower stage of development than the Soviet Union. But does this necessarily mean that more despotic measures must inevitably be used? After all, I would urge, there are several other countries—Rumania and Bulgaria, for example— which are in a similar stage. Or take the countries which are more highly developed, such as East Germany or Poland. If you took the "socialist awareness" that the Albanians claimed was a precondition for Communist success, things looked much less favorable in this regard for the Communists in those two countries than they did in Albania. Only a tiny minority of Poles are convinced of the truth and validity of Communist ideas. The flow of refugees from East Germany, until it was stopped on August 13, 1961, demonstrated how little love the broad masses in that country had for the Communist regime. And yet the leaders of these countries, together with the other satellite leaders, had shifted over to the Kremlin's new course. It does not seem to have done them any harm.

On the contrary, I would ask, would it not in fact increase the chances of success for the Communist system if its representatives gave up their brutal methods and absolute despotism? Might not a policy of the velvet glove, linked with firm ties to the Soviet Union, be more likely to achieve the desired results in the long run than the risky business of an alliance with the far-away Chinese, whose strength is still problematical?

The Albanians would invariably reply to this with a condescending smile. I was correct up to a point, they would say, but I was overlooking another most essential matter. The Albanian Communists' assertion that Stalinism was unavoidable in the current stage of development was paralleled by another factor, which could only formally be separated from the first, since both stood in direct relation to one another. The compulsion to maintain a rigorous internal policy ran parallel to the compulsion to maintain an equally rigorous foreign policy, caused by the "encirclement" of Albania, geographically isolated from the Eastern bloc, by "hostile powers."

Tirana and Yugoslav Revisionism

Another assertion that was often made when the subject of Albania's change of course was under discussion was that it was impossible to understand the country's present thinking without bearing in mind its relations with Yugoslavia. This was something I had no doubt about during my travels in Albania. The Western reader can have no conception of the sheer volume of anti-Yugoslav propaganda that is to be found on placards, posters, and in all other publicity media throughout the country. Not even the "capitalist" or the "imperialist" takes pride of place over the "Titoist" as the "arch-enemy of the nation."

This propaganda is particularly intensive on the country's borders. The walls of the Party Center in Scutari, for example, are covered with huge caricatures mocking the Yugoslav leaders. One of them depicts a bloated Tito on spindly legs in company with a tattered old man who bears the unmistakable features of Uncle Sam, creeping along the outside of a stout wall inscribed "The Socialist Camp." The caption reads "Not a crack to be seen anywhere"—although in view of what I had seen going on in Albania, I found the precise point of this hard to grasp. Posters and streamers along the streets, in factories, and across the fronts of houses and public buildings condemn "revisionist ideas."

The Albanian leaders are, of course, fully aware that the great mass of the people has not the slightest understanding of the abstractions of Communist theory. Instead, the Government exploits the traditional national sentiments. Of the nearly 2½ million Albanians in the Balkans, nearly one million live in the regions of Albania bordering on Yugoslavia. The Communists never tire of giving their subjects harrowing descriptions of the way their compatriots in Yugoslavia are being oppressed and harried.

The simple peasants living in the mountains have no difficulty believing this, for are not the wicked Serbs the ones who for centuries have been coming over the mountains to steal their cattle?

"Revelations" on the misdeeds of the Yugoslavs are made known in books, brochures, and pamphlets. The bookstores of Tirana carry large stocks of these, including some in foreign languages. For example, a booklet in Russian, entitled *In the Prisons and Concentration Camps of Yugoslavia,* gives a detailed account of the criminal activities of the Yugoslav police, which the reader would find hard to distinguish from the crimes committed in the German Third Reich. Every variety of sadistic practice is described, from flogging to forced labor, carried out by starving and naked prisoners in rain and snow. Hundreds of names are quoted to testify to the "authenticity" of the contents.

Another booklet, written in French, contains a series of articles on Yugoslav revisionism. The highspot of the booklet is contained in two newspaper reports, one taken from *The New York Times,* entitled "The Harlem of Belgrade," which describes the wretched condition of Albanians living in the Yugoslav capital. The other is a report by the Belgrade correspondent of the official Chinese news agency describing his experiences during a trip through the Kossovo area of South Yugoslavia, which is inhabited by Albanians.

Pride of place, however, is invariably given to reports of the trials of "agents of the Titoist clique." These are intended not only to demonstrate the hostile attitude of the Yugoslav government toward Albania and the measures of oppression taken against the Albanians living in Yugoslav territory, but even more to make it clear that the Yugoslav Communists are out to wipe an independent Albania off the face of the earth. The press regularly publishes reports on "diversionists," agents, and spies who have crossed the borders with orders to carry out operations against the Albanian state.

There is another intention behind this forced-draught, anti-Yugoslav campaign on the part of the Albanian leaders. This was evident by the number of uniforms I saw everywhere, and by the sight of old men and women showing up for semimilitary training in the streets of Scutari. Armed civilian sentries, for example, are also posted at the entrances to the collective farms, carbines at the ready.

When Communists talk about "increased vigilance" or "encirclement by the enemy," the Western observer becomes suspicious, for he has not yet forgotten Stalin and his methods. Not all civilians are armed in Albania's border regions, and in practice the motto quoted earlier should in all probability be reformulated to read, "The pickaxe for all, but the rifle only for him who can be trusted." There are other indications that show even more clearly that the "vigilance" is directed at the Albanian people more than at the hostile Yugoslavs next door. Night after night, searchlights sweep over the country's bays and harbors from the Yugoslav to the Greek borders, and coastal shipping has been reduced to a minimum by official decree, even though this means using the much more expensive method of transport by land. The quays of the tiny harbors are manned by sentries, whose machine pistols are directed at the few miserable boats and barges tied up in the harbors. On the edge of the Scutari Lake armed patrol boats, disguised as fishing vessels, lie in wait for any vessel that may have the temerity to cross the frontier, which runs through the middle of the lake. The real reason for Albania's deliberate self-isolation and the downright hysterical campaign against "diversionists and spies" is made plain by the barbed wire, the lookout towers, and the strips of forbidden territory along the Albanian frontiers. In this respect, Albania is no different from the other East European countries under Communist domination. Here, too, the border defenses of the Communist paradise are directed more against attack from within than attack from outside.

Still, there can be no doubt that there is some infiltration from the Yugoslav side of the frontier. As far as the North Albanian mountain area is concerned, it is impossible to seal off every one of the desolate mountain tracks. There are Albanians living on both sides of the demarcation line. They have been interconnected by race and family since the beginning of time, so that when Albanians want to cross the frontier in this part of the world, it is not for political reasons. Once their illegal visits to their relatives are ended, most of them return to their homes the same way they came. But however harmless these trips seem to be—and no doubt are—the glowering Tirana officials see dangerous political motives behind them. If Albanians from both sides of the frontier are allowed to get together and swap ideas, there is no knowing what subversive thoughts may not creep into Albania. What, for instance, if the Albanians from the Yugoslav side should tell their relatives on the other side that life in Yugoslavia is freer and less restricted than in Albania, that you are not forced to collectivize your farms or pushed into other compulsory forms of association, that you are allowed to criticize the regime without the risk of going straight to jail or a concentration camp? All this despite the fact that both countries wear the same Communist tag? The fact is that Tito, with his diversionist and more liberal conception of socialism, represents a deadly threat to the terrorist regime in Albania. This is why the Albanian Communists believe that the possibility that "revisionist ideas" might seep into the country must be countered at all costs.

My conversations with Albanian functionaries led me to believe that it is this fear of Yugoslav Communist concepts that is the real reason for the anti-Yugoslav campaign. Although no opportunity is missed to present Yugoslavia as a threat to the very existence of the Albanian nation, the people can never quite bring themselves to believe it. In the past, Albania's membership in the Warsaw Pact made them feel safe against attack. Then again, Soviet arms deliveries, the presence of Soviet military experts, and the Soviet naval units in the Bay of Valona made military or political action by Yugoslavia seem highly unlikely.

Since the end of 1961, of course, the situation has changed. There are continual rumors that the Yugoslavs are preparing to build up a partisan army of Albanian volunteers, to be led by the former prominent Albanian Communist Panajot Plaku. After his flight from Albania in 1957, Plaku said in a statement that he had given the reasons for his flight in a document which he had sent to the Central Committee of the Soviet Communist Party in Moscow. Enver Hoxha thereupon made it known that Khrushchev had offered the Albanian rebel political asylum in the Soviet Union. The fact that Plaku did not accept that offer astonished the Albanian Communists; they suspected that Plaku remained with the Albanian element in South Yugoslavia because he was planning some action against the Albanian government.

The fear of a *coup d'état* from outside the country, on the other hand, has assumed real proportions, although Tirana seems to think that a *Putsch* under present conditions would be based on "revisionist" considerations, and not on any national or political ambitions by Belgrade. There would otherwise be little point in another argument that the Albanian Communists put forward—that they have never made any territorial demands on Yugoslavia.

Speeches and newspaper articles by prominent Albanian functionaries repeatedly stress that Albania does not demand any "corrections of the frontier," but only that Albanians living in Kossovo, Macedonia, and Metohija should be allowed to live in conditions worthy of human beings. However, these statements do not really chime with the fact that the Albanian Government is prepared to use any possible means to whip up the nationalistic sentiments of the people, thus showing that what Tirana wants to achieve is a clean break. It is said that the main thing in the anti-Yugoslav campaign is not the nationalistic standpoint, but the Leninist concept of "proletarian internationalism." The real consideration, in other words, is not chauvinism but "the maintenance of the purity of the Teaching." The Albanian Communists, I was assured, are the truly upright vanguard in the fight being waged by the international proletariat, while the Titoist revisionists are in reality "imperialist exploiters" of the worst kind, as is proved by the oppression of the Albanian minority in South Yugoslavia. It is the attitude demonstrated by arguments like this that lead one to the conclusion that at the root of Albania's hostility to Yugoslavia lies, not so much anxiety about an attack on the country's actual territory, as the fear of ideological infection. This is also the reason why the Albanians so strenuously resist any rise in Yugoslavia's standing within the Eastern bloc, since they feel it would automatically endanger the position of the Albanian leaders. It explains Albania's uneasiness at the Kremlin's efforts to achieve reconciliation between Moscow and Belgrade, and their mistrust of the fast-talking and slippery Khrushchev. This mistrust is the reason why Albanian propaganda stopped mentioning Khrushchev's name long before the actual conflict. The Albanian leaders must have felt aggrieved at the fact that it was Khrushchev who took the initiative in trying to bring about a reconciliation with Tito.

At the Red summit meeting in Moscow in November, 1960, Enver Hoxha indignantly demanded to know why there had been so many meetings in Brioni and none in Albania. This was a reference to the fact that Khrushchev's first visit to Yugoslavia had been in 1955, whereas he did not get around to making the trip to the still-faithful Albania until 1959.

In November, 1961, Hoxha revealed another circumstance which throws still more light on Albania's growing resentment at the attempts to bring about an understanding between the Soviets and Yugoslavia. He read aloud parts of a letter which Khrushchev had sent to Tito on November 9, 1956, which was made known to the Albanian Government by Krylov, then Soviet Ambassador in Tirana. From this letter it emerged that even before the revolt in Hungary, Khrushchev and Tito had come to the conclusion that Rakosi, for many years the head man in the Hungarian Communist Party, would have to be deposed, and replaced by Janos Kadar. Hoxha argued that one could not do two diametrically opposite things at the same time: to consult with Tito on an important matter, such as filling the post of a Party leader in a neighboring Communist country, was simply incompatible with simultaneously reproaching Tito in a blaze of publicity for his revisionist views. These remarks by Hoxha were a clear reflection of his fear that one day Khrushchev and Tito might again consult together, this time to decide on a successor to Hoxha himself! This anxiety of Hoxha's was not made any less by the fact that in April, 1956, the Kremlin, as Hoxha also revealed in the same speech, had commissioned Suslov and Pospelov to try to persuade the Albanian Party to rehabilitate Kochi Xoxe, who had been executed in 1948, for his alleged "Titoism."

The Albanians' mistrust of Khrushchev was only increased by other remarks he made. In September, 1961, for example, in a *New York Times* interview, he declared that the Kremlin "of course" regarded Yugoslavia as a socialist country. This statement was equivalent to a revaluation of Tito of a kind that must have made the Albanian Communists feel their position to be highly disagreeable, not to say dangerous. Hoxha was not entirely wrong when he attacked Khrushchev's ambiguous policy at the Moscow meeting in November, 1960, with the words, "The revisionists of Honolulu have been unmasked, but not those in Belgrade."

This and similar reactions by Tirana indicate how much the Albanian Communists tend to draw a parallel between the reformist activities Khrushchev has been engaged in since the Twentieth Party Congress—which the Albanians have been following with growing uneasiness—and the revisionist ideas of the Yugoslavs. They have been increasingly worried that the machinations of the Soviets and Yugoslavs might one day reach into Albania and over-turn the existing political power structure. It seems clear that the Albanians would not have gone into action as they did if they had not felt there was good reason for it. In 1960, the Kremlin decided on certain foreign policy moves which threatened to upset the balance of power in the Balkans, and would have directly affected Albania. It is not to be wondered at that Moscow's surprise move in the Balkans caused a no less surprising reaction on the part of Tirana, the first indication of the sensational change of course that was to come later.

The Kremlin's New Balkan Policy

The conditions I had seen in the Albanian-Yugoslav border region were almost exactly duplicated in the far south of the coun-try, in the part the Greeks call North Epirus *Irredenta*. For the Albanian Communists, the south is just as much in danger as the north, since Greece, just like the "arch-enemy" Yugoslavia, is seen as one of the countries forming the "hostile encirclement" of which Tirana has been complaining for years. The difference is only one of degree.

Soldiers and police are everywhere, and barriers and check-points bar most roads. Along the line of the frontier are the usual barbed-wire entanglements, the look-out towers, and the dead man's strip. Here, too, are the familiar armed civilians—I even saw "anglers" who hastily covered up their weapons as I ap-proached. The explanation is, of course, that the "spies and diver-sionists," trying to penetrate Albanian soil from all sides, are the cause of all this. When my escort observed that the sentries were much more numerous than when he had last been in this part of the country, it did not take him long to think up the reason. In the last treason trial in Tirana, it had been "revealed" that a large number of acts of sabotage had been committed just about here. A few days later, an Albanian Communist functionary told me that "subversive elements" had been caught near Koritza, one of them having been killed in the struggle to capture them. It turned out that this man had only come across the border from Greece a few days before, and had been identified as a prominent member of the former group of quislings who had been tolerated as the "government" by the Germans during the war.

More instructive still than all the stories about "spies" and "subversive elements" was my trip along the Greek frontier from Argyrocastro to Leskovik. Needless to say, no Albanian may travel this route without special permission. The barbed-wire entanglements in the river along the border, the dead man's strip, the numerous watchtowers, and the innumerable checks by Albanian military control points were all symptoms of political hysteria. We had the greatest difficulty in getting past the controls, in spite of the bundle of special passes my escort had been given by the authorities in Tirana and Argyrocastro. At the most important control point, a few hundred yards from the Greek border, the sentry vanished into the checkpoint building with all our papers and did not reappear for a long time, the time it took to clear everything to his satisfaction.

All in all, it looked to me as though the controls and checking measures in the south were every bit as rigid as those in the north, if not in fact worse. I could not decide whether it was because the people here were more hostile to the regime than their compatriots near the Yugoslav frontier, or whether they were considered more likely to want to flee the country. One thing was certainly noticeable. I seldom met anyone in Albania who appeared happy and relaxed in the enjoyment of his "freedom and independence," but here in the south there seemed to be an atmosphere of downright dejection. The people looked more care-worn here than elsewhere.

Another very peculiar item seemed to require explanation. Argyrocastro is the birthplace of Enver Hoxha. But when I asked to be taken to the house where he was born, all I found was a heap of rubble, with a wretched-looking monument nearby recording the fact that this really was Hoxha's birthplace. In reply to my question as to the reason for this condition of the house, I was told it had been hit by a bomb during the war. But this was twenty years ago, time enough for the "leader's" birthplace to be restored. It could even have become a kind of shrine, as Stalin's birthplace had become in Russia. My remarks were met with silence. Not even the favorite argument about the abolition of the cult of personality in Albania was brought forth. There was some mumbled phrase to the effect that the house would be rebuilt "soon," but there was no sign of any preparations for it.

While I do not claim that any concrete conclusions about the state of political affairs in South Albania can be drawn from these few indications, there is probably some basis for the particularly stringent security precautions being applied there. The leaders in Tirana may well have to face action from the Greeks as well as from the Yugoslavs. Minorities are always a delicate subject, particularly those living in strongly nationalist states under totalitarian rule. Moreover, Athens has said for years that when the Cyprus question was out of the way, the Greek Government would energetically tackle the matter of North Epirus, and there is little doubt that the Greek population of southern Albania has been following the Greek Government's intentions with both interest and sympathy.

The Albanian leaders were made very angry by something that happened in June, 1960, and in which Khrushchev played a direct part. The Greek Liberal leader Venizelos was on a visit to the Soviet Union, and Khrushchev granted him an interview. According to the Athens newspaper *To Vima*, Venizelos told Khrushchev of the Greek Government's concern over the North Epirus question, and asked him to support Athens' attempt to achieve autonomy for North Epirus. Khrushchev promised to bring up this point at the Rumanian Party Congress in Bucharest on June 20, to which all the East European Communist leaders had been called. This may have been one of the reasons why Hoxha did not appear at this meeting himself, but sent his third-in-line man, Hysni Kapo. Hoxha dealt later with this Venizelos interview, which in the meantime had caused widespread attention, when he stated at the Moscow meeting, in November, that Albania would never agree to "any territorial concessions." "We have given Mr. Sophocles Venizelos the answers he deserves," he went on, not only indicating the Albanian position on the Greek demands, but also stating his opinion of Khrushchev's promise.

However, Krushchev's promise to the Greek Liberal leader was only one item in the totality of the strategy the Kremlin was beginning to apply in the Balkans, a strategy which had for some time contained a "peace offensive" as one of its components. As long as this "peace" drive showed clear propaganda features, the Albanians had no objections to it. But this Venizelos interview made the Albanians wonder if Moscow was thinking of underlining the Soviet "peace offensive" by ignoring or even damaging Albania's interests. From this time on, there was unmistakable evidence of a split between Moscow and the Soviet satellites on the one hand, and Albania on the other, in regard to the Eastern bloc's Balkan policy.

The Soviets had made a number of attempts to weaken the South-East cornerstone of the NATO system. The objects of these efforts were Greece and Turkey, and the instruments were Rumania and Bulgaria, who had long been supported by Albania. The Soviet-Balkan peace offensive started at the same time as the Rapacki Plan was put up for consideration in East Germany. The initiative in proposing an easing of tension, and later a denuclearized zone in the Balkans, came from Rumania; the East bloc's suggestion, when it was published in September, 1957, bore the name of the Rumanian Prime Minister Chivu Stoica. The Stoica Plan, addressed to the Bulgarian, Albanian, Greek, Turkish, and Yugoslav governments, proposed that there should be a summit conference of all these states to discuss outstanding differences, and thus pave the way for a general relaxation of tension in the Balkans. As might have been expected, Bulgaria and Albania supported the proposal. Yugoslavia also agreed in principle, but did not think a summit conference along the lines suggested would be helpful at this time. Greece and Turkey rejected the proposal, the Greeks adding that they could not see the plan being realized in the foreseeable future.

This rejection did not prevent the Rumanian Government from pressing on with its efforts and starting up a large-scale propaganda campaign, supported by Bulgaria and Albania and, eventually, by the Soviet Union. But the chances of success grew dimmer. Relations with Yugoslavia hit bottom when Tito published his new "revisionist" Party program at the Seventh Yugoslav Party Congress, and was immediately subjected to violent abuse by the other Eastern-bloc countries. Then, when the Greeks and Turks decided to set up NATO rocket bases on their territory, the squabble with the Yugoslav Communists took second place for a while, and a fresh move was made.

In June, 1959, Stoica renewed his invitation to a Balkan summit conference. This time the agenda was tailored to the current situation. The main items were to be the creation of a "peace zone" and the outlawing of all rocket bases and nuclear weapons in the Balkans. The guiding hand behind the Rumanian proposal was even more obvious than before. Khrushchev had visited Albania in May and June, 1959, and the speeches he had made in the course of his visit had been full of threats against Greece and Turkey. Accordingly, the "negotiations" had had ample preparation. It was not surprising that the second Stoica proposal should be cordially welcomed in the Kremlin. Albania and Bulgaria supported the Rumanians. Tito once more gave his agreement in principle, but objected that a conference would not do away with the danger of an atomic war in the area of the Balkans. Greece rejected the proposal, and Turkey did not even reply.

Following on this fiasco, the Soviets tried another tack. There seemed to be no point in addressing the Greek and Turkish governments directly, but the Soviets believed that a propaganda campaign beamed at the Balkan peoples might prove more effective. At the end of June, 1959, a Soviet Government announcement called for the creation of a denuclearized zone in the Balkans and on the Adriatic. Although the inclusion of the Adriatic seemed to imply that Italy was also thought of in this context, the main effort was directed at influencing Greece. Rumania was accordingly pulled out of the propaganda front line and replaced by Bulgaria, Greece's immediate northern neighbor. A wave of Communist propaganda rolled over the Balkan NATO partner. In

August of that year, the Bulgarians offered to conclude a nonaggression pact with Greece. The Greeks declined, and their refusal was greeted with a storm of indignation in Sofia and Bucharest—and in Tirana.

The Albanians seemed to have been full of enthusiasm for the Soviets' efforts to achieve an easing of tension in the Balkans. Mehmet Shehu, Albanian Prime Minister, confirmed in the official Bulgarian Party paper *Rabotnitchesko Delo* that he welcomed the Bulgarians' efforts. Moreover, he said, he regarded the plan as "very realistic."

Despite the unequivocal nature of the Greek reply, the Bulgarians continued their offensive. The primary target of their attacks was the "reactionary government," which was refusing to accede to the "most ardent longings" of its own people. It was in this context that the Bulgarian Party leader Shivkoff gave an interview to the Greek Communist journal *Avgi* in December, 1959, claiming that Greek public opinion was increasingly opposed to the Greek Government's foreign policy. The Greek Government, he claimed, did not want to keep step with the movement in the international situation "in the direction of peace and mutual understanding." These Bulgarian claims were accompanied by massive threats. Bulgaria, it was pointed out, did not have any rocket bases and did not want any: But if such bases were to be established in neighboring countries, Bulgaria would have no alternative but to do the same. This general propaganda line was continued right up to the beginning of 1960, during which period the Albanian Communist leaders made speeches and issued declarations in support of the standpoint of their Bulgarian, Rumanian, and, in particular, their Soviet comrades.

Then came the change. Khrushchev's interview with Venizelos had already alerted Tirana, and before long their fears were to increase. At the beginning of September, the Bulgarian Prime Minister, Anton Jugoff, in an interview with the Athens paper *To Vima*, touched on the question of regional disarmament in the Balkans. Bulgaria, he said, had already made two separate reductions in the size of her forces, but she was ready to go still further, provided she could reach agreement with her neighbors, to effect total disarmament in this part of Europe.

This interview sparked off a display of temper in the Albanian capital, although this was mixed with a certain amount of doubt about what Jugoff had really meant, with respect to the period of time involved and the way of carrying out the projected disarmament. All doubts were removed, however, when, on September 28, Party leader Shivkoff gave precise details of the Bulgarian disarmament proposals before the United Nations in New York. Unfortunately, so he told the General Assembly, all the plans of the Bulgarian and Rumanian governments to ease tension in the Balkans had come to nothing. However, his Government was ready to go even further. He suggested that the Balkan countries should reduce their forces to the point where all that would be left, in effect, would be frontier guards. The Balkans, he said, should become the first area to put into effect the Eastern bloc's idea of global total disarmament.

In the West, there was much discussion of Shivkoff's real intention in proposing total disarmament in the Balkans. Shivkoff's thought probably was that if agreement on general and total disarmament were to be reached—as Khrushchev had proposed to the United Nations General Assembly—the implementation could be started in the Balkans, which would have to be followed by world-wide disarmament. It is unlikely that Shivkoff was inspired by the hope that total disarmament in the Balkans would in itself set in motion disarmament by the rest of the world.

Whatever the truth of the matter may be, the Albanian Communists immediately saw that Shivkoff's proposal contained a completely new element, and they sensed a threat to the stability of their regime. On his return from the U.N. meeting, Prime Minister Mehmet Shehu told the Albanian National Assembly that no idea of total, regional disarmament "conceived in any Balkan brain" would ever be acceptable. The suggestion that the Balkan countries should disarm down to purely defensive border guards, at a time when rocket bases were being built in Italy, and the United States Sixth Fleet was lying in wait in the Adriatic like "a dragon with wide-open jaws," was both absurd and dangerous to any socialist country in the Balkans. The realization of such a plan would mean that the socialist country concerned would allow its national existence to become dependent on the favor of the "imperialist wolves." General and total disarmament must never be carried out in the Balkans before it has taken place in other parts of the world. The best thing, Shehu concluded, would be for all nations to start disarming simultaneously, in accordance with the conditions suggested by the Soviet Union.

The Albanian Communists reacted with similar asperity to another proposal—this time one that Poland had put forward at the United Nations General Assembly. The Polish leader Gomulka had suggested that no new military bases should be established by any nation on the territory of another country. Shehu rejected this proposal. Albania, he said, could not agree to the maintenance of the *status quo* in regard to existing military bases. That would simply imply the acceptance of the existing situation, in which "hundreds of American military bases encircle the Socialist camp." In fact, it would imply willingness to legalize this situation, despite the fact that these bases were known to represent a grave danger to the security of the socialist states. Gomulka's proposal would therefore do nothing toward ensuring peace. On the contrary, it would be as good as provoking the "imperialist aggressors" to undertake "fresh acts of military aggression."

At the end of 1960, the Albanian Communists had made it clear before the whole world that on certain points they refused to go along with the foreign-policy strategy of the Eastern bloc. Since it was unlikely that either Bulgaria or Poland would have made its moves in the U.N. without the agreement and support of Moscow, Tirana's charges were mainly directed against the Soviets. A more unanimous policy by all the Communist Balkan states against Greece and Turkey, with the vigorous assistance of the Soviet Union, was no longer possible. As long as they were dealing with proposals that remained within certain limits, the Communist countries were in agreement with each other. The outlawing of nuclear weapons and rocket bases, the peace campaign, and nonagression pacts—these were things the Albanians could go along with. But the outlawing of nuclear weapons and the signing of nonaggression pacts are not equivalent to total regional disarmament. As long as disarmament proposals such as Khrushchev's remained within general, theoretical, and propaganda bounds, Tirana could accept them. More concrete plans, that would have had a much more direct effect on Albania, were rejected.

It may be objected that neither Khrushchev's proposal nor that of Shivkoff is likely to have been anything more than a shot in the propaganda battle. This would illustrate even more clearly the ingrained mistrust and skepticism the Albanians felt toward any measures or suggestions by their Communist allies that appeared to contain even a suggestion of danger to the Albanian regime. Khrushchev's interview with Venizelos, and the statements by Shivkoff and Gomulka in New York, had so alarmed the Albanians that they were not willing to take any chances.

From the middle of 1960 on, Albania was beset by another fear in addition to the smoldering differences in regard to fundamental Communist Party policy, domestic arrangements, and the worry over the Yugoslav revisionists: It is the fear that the Soviets might be prepared, as part of their policy of peaceful coexistence, to agree to concessions which would not do them any harm, but might turn out to be at the expense of Albania. The Albanians were afraid that if any such Kremlin foreign-policy maneuver in the Balkans were to be successful, it might have disastrous consequences for the internal situation of their country. So there is some reason to think that the immediate cause of Albania's switch of political course was Moscow's Balkan policy, at a time when the first signs of the break-up of international Communism were making themselves evident.

Enver for All and All for Enver!

The objective observer may well feel that the Albanian Communists' suspicion of Moscow was justified; yet the final revolt would not be entirely comprehensible without consideration of another essential factor. At bottom, the cause of Albania's break with Moscow was the Albanian Communists' theories on how the existing governmental structure should be maintained. These decided views on the part of the Albanian leaders were conditioned by their characters and mentalities, which must be examined in order to reach a better understanding of political developments in Albania.

As in all totalitarian states, the personality and character of the top man play a decisive role. In no other East European state has one man molded the national Communist Party so definitely in the last twenty years as in Albania. The slogan "Enver Hoxha is the Party and the Party is Enver Hoxha" is confirmed wherever one goes. Hoxha is everywhere; nobody can escape his ubiquitous presence, whether in town or village. In the public gardens, there are golden busts of him between the palm fronds or the eucalyptus leaves. On the public square or in front of government buildings, his image in bronze or plaster watches over the activities of his subjects. His portrait, well or badly painted, can be found in the most unlikely places. To have the dictator's picture in every tavern and hotel, and in all schools and ministries, is in line with normal custom in all totalitarian countries. But to see Enver alongside the sleazy beer tent on the beach, on a pennant at the edge of the football field, or decorating an archeological collection in a provincial museum—that goes even further than just bad taste. The Party propagandists seem to seek out every uncovered piece of wall in the inhabited areas to mount their hero's picture. Even the walls of the cowsheds in the collective farms and the windows of the meagerly stocked town shops are not spared. Furthermore, organized groups are ready to chant his name whenever the slightest opportunity is offered.

Who is this Enver Hoxha, the man who, for all the condemnation of the "cult of personality," allows himself to be adulated as no other Communist leader has dared to do for years? Who is this man who, at the Party Congress in February, 1961, produced an orgy of self-praise that not even Stalin could have bettered? In front of colossal portraits of the great men of Communism—Marx, Engels, Lenin, and Stalin—Hoxha hurled his theses into the auditorium. A few yards behind him a gleaming plaster bust of himself towered above him.

On this evidence, Enver Hoxha is a man whose outstanding characteristics must be arrogance and the lust for power. But in a number of ways, Hoxha is remarkably unlike the rulers of other Communist countries. Tall, athletic, upright, and with a springy step, he is an impressive figure. When he appears in the colorful uniform of a General of the Army, he looks the very incarnation of the cool and valorous popular hero who is bound to fascinate the Albanian man in the street. Even in civilian clothes, he is still what is known as a "fine figure" of a man. His face, with its broad, frank smile, is attractive. His eyes are cold and brilliant, their lively glance, like the high forehead, attesting to his intelligence. He is fluent in several languages.

The fifty-five-year old dictator comes of a middle-class Mohammedan family from Argyrocastro. He was brought up in comfortable circumstances, attended high school in Koritza, and in 1930, won a state scholarship to the science faculty of Montpellier University in France. It was here that he first became interested in politics. In spite of his intelligence and his flair for languages, his scholarship was withdrawn after only one year on the grounds of lack of effort.

Hoxha then moved to Paris, where he came under the influence of the French left-wing intellectuals. He was taken under the wing of Valliant Couturier, at that time the publisher of the French Communist paper *L'Humanité*. In the company of the small group of left-wing Albanian students and the gifted émigré Lazar Fundo, he took his first steps along the road of Communist ideology. Lack of money forced him to go to Brussels, where the honorary Albanian consul had offered him a job as his private secretary. Hoxha studied law in his spare time, but never got as far as qualifying.

After six years in Western Europe, Hoxha returned to Albania. The East European comrades have never been quite happy about those six years in the West—Stalin, for example, never trusted Hoxha. Dedijer's biography of Tito contains several mentions of Stalin's repeated questions to the Yugoslav dictator on his opinion of Hoxha, and whether he would remain loyal to the cause. Molotov, who had first met Hoxha in Paris, praised his wide learning, but qualified this opinion by immediately adding that you could feel the influence of his Western education. Kardelj, presently the chief ideological expert of the Yugoslav Party, told Stalin during the period of Albanian-Yugoslav friendship that Hoxha possessed certain "petty-bourgeois traits" and did not have a complete "correct Marxist-Leninist training."

These doubts in the minds of the other Communists may well have been justified, but for all that, Hoxha has qualities that fit him for the "dictatorship of the proletariat" much more than working-class origin or intensive Communist indoctrination alone would do. From the very beginning, he understood that the realization of Communist rule is a matter of power. In the past two decades, he has proven that he is at home with power, that he knows how to wield it, and that he is determined to let nobody wrest it from him.

When Hoxha returned home, he found Albania virtually unchanged. The country still had no industries to speak of, and the majority of the people were still illiterate. No other European country was so far removed from the conditions Marx had said were necessary for a Communist revolution. The few Albanians who were at all interested in politics were well left of center, but it was difficult to find any points of common agreement to weld them together. The intellectuals, most of whom had studied abroad, were pained by the backwardness of their country and thought that radical improvement could only be brought about by a violent revolution. How this revolution was to be set in motion and on what basis—there, opinions differed widely. For many people, the focal point of their thinking lay in the loss of Kossovo to Yugoslavia, and some saw a means of recovering the area in Lenin's acknowledgment of the right of all peoples to self-determination. The same argument led others to embrace Fascism, because they had heard of Mussolini's attacks on "pan-Serbian attempts at expansion."

These left-orientated groups, with their widely divergent aims, played a less important part in the development of Communism in Albania than politically enlightened Albanians in exile. When Achmed Zogu toppled Bishop Fan Noli's Government, Fan Noli and other politicians and intellectuals emigrated. They spread over the whole of Europe, but they did form a "National Committee" in Vienna, founded by Fan Noli and a few of the members of the former Tirana Government. The difficulties and disappointments of their émigré existence, and above all their complete lack of funds, eventually led to their falling under the influence of Moscow. Those who opposed this development were expelled. Following this "purge," the National Committee assumed the new title of "National Liberation," and took up contact with the Comintern in Moscow.

To begin with, the National Liberation group had no actual influence on internal developments within Albania, but it did become an important meeting point for Albanian Communist-sympathizers who had left their homeland. They not only received guidance from the Comintern, but were also given ideological and political training in Party schools in Moscow. At the end of 1930, the Comintern decided to send home several Moscow-trained Albanians to do propaganda work among isolated left-wing elements in their country, and to start up well-founded and well-organized political activity.

The most important and effective Comintern agent among the returning émigrés was Ali Kelmendi, an ex-NCO in the Albanian police, who had gone to Moscow after the fall of Fan Noli. He was only of mediocre intelligence, but possessed tremendous energy. He made a start on building up Communist groups in Tirana, Koritza, and Scutari.

Of these three, the one in Koritza seemed likely to be most successful. This go-ahead town had a French high school, with a staff of teachers who were in sympathy with "progressive" political ideas, and who thus provided a nucleus of political agitation. In a certain sense, the French high school in Koritza can be regarded as the spiritual starting point of Communism in Albania, in that a number of socialist professors from Paris guided the young Albanian intellectuals along the road leading to the world of Marxist theory, a fact that proved most useful to Kelmendi. Not that the first and most important of the Communist cells was very large. Before World War II, it never had more than seventy members, and it was both rudimentary in structure and hazy in its ideas. Nevertheless, it was able to link up with socialist or Communist auxiliary organizations and workers' associations in other countries.

However, the scanty initial success of the Communist cells in Albania were not destined to continue for long. In the year that

Enver Hoxha returned home from the West, the Albanian Communists lost their leading man. In 1936, Kelmendi, who had been under ceaseless observation by Zog's government agents for a considerable time, decided he had better give up undercover work; he fled to Greece to escape the net that was being drawn ever closer around him. Internal strife immediately broke out among the Communist cells, each accusing the other of left-wing or right-wing deviationism. One would be suspected of Trotskyism, another of Bukharinism, while each of them claimed to be the only true upholder of Albanian Communism and Marxism-Leninism. All this took place at the time of the great Moscow purges.

By 1937, the Comintern thought it was time to put an end to this self-laceration by the handful of Albanian Communists and ordered that all existing groups should be dissolved. The Communist movement in Albania was to be reorganized and given a new set of leaders who knew their exact aims, who would not spend most of their time suspecting and accusing other members of the movement, and who would steadfastly work to spread Communism among the masses. As might have been expected, these Comintern directives never got beyond the paper stage, since, although the Party was reorganized, the leaders were the same, and everything went on as before.

The only one who did not join in the general backbiting between the individual Communist groups was Enver Hoxha, and he energetically set to work to propagate the theme of unity and agreement within the movement. He had originally settled in Tirana on his return, but soon realized that the Koritza cell offered the best chance both of spreading Communist doctrine and improving his own position within the Party. He therefore moved to Koritza, and took a job as a teacher in the French high school. He was still too young and unknown to be able to force his ideas through despite opposition from the older Communists, but his unflagging support for the idea of unity among the Albanian Communists paved the way for his eventual rise in the Communist ranks.

The Italian invasion in 1939 gave Hoxha his opportunity. Left-wing émigrés were returning to their homeland and doing their best to stoke up the fires of Albanian patriotism. Hoxha increased his efforts to coordinate the work of the Communist groups. Thus when he moved from Koritza to Tirana in 1940, and opened a cigar store, it soon became the center of Communist activity. The first sabotage operation against the Italians was organized, several supply depots were set on fire, and a number of police informers murdered; but the general run of these first operations was of no great importance. Hoxha and his handful of supporters were too busy organizing the long-overdue basic policy conferences between the various Communist groups, particularly those in Koritza, Tirana, and Scutari. Neither the standing nor the influence of the ambitious cigar dealer was yet great enough to enable him to get his way. Political collaboration, even when agreed between the leading personalities, always ran aground on the continual personal differences between individuals.

The Albanian Communists lacked a leading personality with enough authority to build up and hold together an organization in this favorable situation of 1939 and 1940. There were two men who might have achieved it, but their time was past. Ali Kelmendi, the Comintern agent, the most effectual organizer so far, had died of tuberculosis in Paris in 1939. Shortly before his death, he had blocked the path of another Albanian Communist leader when he expelled Lazar Fundo, Hoxha's former mentor, from the Party for "bourgeois deviationism" in 1938. Fundo was called to Moscow to explain and was condemned to death, which he escaped only because of Georgi Dimitrov's intercession. He later returned to Albania, but his reputation had been so tarnished that he stood no chance of being able to smooth out the rivalries between the different groups.

The only way out of this situation was to call in help from outside the country. The Yugoslav Party had for a long time felt concerned about the fate of their Albanian comrades. After the Italian invasion of Albania, the Yugoslav Communists saw possibilities in the organizing of an effective resistance movement against the Italians, of which they might later be able to make political capital. This was the reason why, in the summer of 1940, the Yugoslav Communists decided on a remarkable organizational measure. The Party organization of the Kossovo-Metohija area, which was inhabited by Albanians, was detached from the Montenegro Provincial Committee and put directly under command of the Central Committee. At the same time, the Kossovo District Committee was charged with working up an effective Communist resistance movement in Albania, a task which was all the more urgent because German forces had moved into Albania in the spring of 1941. The Yugoslav Communists got into touch with their Albanian comrades, something that had been sadly neglected before.

An important part in this contacting was played by the Party secretaries of the Kossovo-Metohija District Committee, Miladin Popovich and Dusan Mugosa, both of whom traveled to Tirana in 1941, and set about trying to weld the various Communist groups into an effective single Party. The difficulties they met in so doing are clear from a report later written by Mugosa. The main task the Yugoslavs were faced with was to bring together the three most important and powerful groups. The oldest and most important was the Koritza cell, to which Hoxha had belonged. It was the cell which seemed to correspond with the Yugoslavian idea of what such a group should be—at least it had something resembling an organization. At the same time, Mugosa reported later, its main activity seemed to be confined to pretty speeches and the confused discussion of a variety of subjects having nothing whatever to do with the most urgent current problem—namely, the organizing of the most effective armed resistance to the occupation authorities.

The second Communist group, the one in Scutari, had not been started until 1938. The leader of this group worked on the principle that no Communist movement could develop fully in Albania as long as the economic situation remained as it had been before the Italians occupied the country. He believed that the action of the Italian imperialists was frankly necessary in order to create a working class and a proletariat. The growth of proletarian awareness would be accelerated by the investment in Albania of foreign capital, and it was only at this later stage that a serious start could be made on spreading Communist ideas.

The way Mugosa described it, the third group, the so-called Youth Group, was more like a circle of dervishes than a disciplined Communist cell. The members were urged to "mortify the

flesh and to hate their families." They had to find the requisite
funds themselves, which they did without scruple, stealing whatever they could lay their hands on and handing the booty to their
group leader. It was no wonder that some extremely sinister characters had managed to join the ranks.

The emissaries from the Yugoslav Party center would never
have achieved their object if they had not angled their approach
in a way that made a profound impression on the Albanian Communists and on those who believed themselves to be such. Their
angle was to confine their efforts, first, to strengthening the Albanians' resistance to the Italians, and, second, to arousing Albanian hopes of being accepted into the Comintern as ideologically respected Party comrades. By using these two arguments,
they managed to damp down the jealousies between the separate
Albanian groups, and to create a unified body that made it possible to build up an effective Party faithful to the Communist line.

On November 8, 1941, twenty members from the separate Albanian cells met in Tirana and formed the Party. The tasks of the
new Party were drawn up in statutes: to train the cadre, to foster
devotion to the Soviet Union, and to carry out propaganda activity
among the workers and peasants by means of patriotic slogans. As
a sign of its unity of action, the newly founded Albanian Communist Party issued a proclamation calling on the Albanian people
to refuse to pay taxes and to revolt against the Italians. The Communists were called on to place themselves in the forefront of the
fight. As a first step, the manifesto recommended boycotting the
Italians, who should be given not even "one grain of corn, one
drop of oil, or one glass of water."

More important than this semi-routine recommendation by the
Party's founding committee was another decision. Enver Hoxha
was nominated Secretary General of the Albanian Communist
Party. Hoxha, who was far superior to his colleagues in intelligence and tactical flair, and who had unfailingly fought for the
unification of the Party and thus gained the confidence of the
Yugoslav Communists and their emissaries at the foundation
conference in Tirana, had succeeded in his plans to become the
leader of the Albanian Communists.

In order to maintain the "unity and purity of the cadre," he began the first of the purges. Trotskyites and other deviationists were "unmasked." Many were expelled from the Party, and a few were executed. The word "discipline" took first place in all the proclamations made by the new Central Committee.

The Yugoslavs as well as Enver Hoxha thought there was much to be gained by carrying on the active struggle against the Italian invaders. The cover of "patriotism" could be used to create political preconditions which would subsequently smooth the path to the take-over of power. The first Communist partisan groups were established at the beginning of 1942. The majority of the cadres left their towns and villages in order to take over command of partisan units in the forests and mountains. The first coordinated military actions took place in July, 1942. Telephone lines were cut in the south, military barracks were set on fire in Koritza, an ammunition depot was blown up in Valona, and the central military supply depot and the telephone installations in Tirana were destroyed. In the summer and fall, the partisans' attacks increased. From the south, where the Communist resistance had originated, the Communist-controlled partisan groups pushed forward into the interior. Toward the end of 1942, the Italians abandoned large areas of the country to the partisans.

But the leaders were not satisfied. At that time, there were no permanent partisan units but only armed peasants, who carried out their actions under the command of a local leader or political commissar. These groups would carry out a sabotage raid or have a short exchange of fire with the enemy, and then return to their work in the fields. What the leaders had in mind was the setting up of tightly knit, organized troop units, which could be sent into action by the Communists. They felt that there must be systematic preparation of the political ground against the day of liberation, against the moment when the occupying forces would disappear, leaving behind a political vacuum. This vacuum would then be filled by well-organized military units under Communist control. To this end, in September, 1942, to the accompaniment of appeals to fraternity and love of the fatherland, an organization was created that to all outward appearances would accommodate the adherents of the various political parties. This Communist-controlled organization was given the high-sounding name of "National Freedom Movement," and in its early days it actually did embrace most of the forces in the country engaged in opposing the Italian occupation.

Meanwhile, in Moscow, Tito had managed to get the Comintern to agree to acknowledge the Albanian Communists. In sending the Albanian comrades this news, Tito added some advice which included recommendations on the organizing of the Party. In his view, the Party ought to be "monolithic," run on the basis of "strict discipline." On this point both Tito and Hoxha were in full agreement, both taking as their starting point the premise that the senior positions in a partisan organization should be filled by Party comrades willing to give unconditional obedience to the orders and instructions of the top leaders. Hoxha meanwhile had been elected General Secretary of the second provisional Central Committee of the Albanian Communist Party, had been given the leadership of the National Freedom Movement, and made commander of the army of this freedom movement. He set to work. Using drastic methods, he saw to it that a "monolithic" command structure in the Albanian partisan units was put into effect.

Events in the summer of 1943 gave new impetus to Hoxha's plans. The defeat of the Axis Powers in Europe was only a matter of time. Mussolini fell, Italy's capitulation was imminent, and the Allied forces were advancing from Sicily in the direction of Rome. The Italians relaxed their grip on Albania. As the Albanians' prospects of victory grew, the National Freedom Movement began to fall apart. Those patriotic Albanians who could read the political signs retired sobered, as they realized that the freedom movement had fallen into the hands of a few Moscow-controlled functionaries, who were using patriotic slogans to cover up their misuse of national, patriotic elements to further their plans for Communist domination.

There were two groups in particular that revolted against the Communists' claim to sole power: the *Legaliteti* in North Albania, which had royalist aims, and the *Balli Kombetar* in the south, which was conservative in character. The leader of the *Legaliteti* was Abas Kupi, the adventurous chief of a Gegh tribe, who had been one of the first to call for resistance to the Italians as early as 1939.

He had been able to gather together a number of Gegh chiefs for united action in the rugged northern mountains, but this did not lead to any regular resistance activity. Kupi's organization had all the earmarks of a gang of political brigands, who found a suitable hunting ground in the wild mountain country, although Kupi himself was admittedly animated by his desire for Albania's freedom and independence. When the National Freedom Movement was formed, Kupi joined it immediately and became one of its ten-man Central Committee. However, his influence was limited. The continual rivalry between the families and tribes made the tribal Gegh chiefs from North Albania unwilling to leave their home ground in order to take part in national political activity. So the control of the National Freedom Movement remained safely in Communist hands.

The second nationalist resistance group, the *Balli Kombetar* (National Front), was founded at the end of 1942 by a few conservative politicians from the south, who managed to form a small number of fighting units. Their demand was that the Kossovo district should become Albanian. In the summer of 1943, both they and the Communists made efforts to bring about closer cooperation between the two organizations in the fight for liberation. In August, negotiations began in the town of Mukaj, finally leading to the creation of a unified organization with the name "National Committee for the Rescue of Albania." The representatives of *Balli Kombetar* won acceptance of their demand to permanently incorporate the Kossovo district into the Albanian state after the final victory. However, when an envoy from Tito, the ranking Yugoslav Communist, Vukmanovic-Tempo, arrived at the Communists' headquarters shortly afterwards, he indignantly repudiated the agreement with *Balli Kombetar*, and demanded that it be canceled in the name of the National Freedom Movement. The Albanian Communists bowed down and obeyed. In an attempt to put a new face on their submission, they accompanied it by a series of accusations against *Balli Kombetar*.

This episode illustrates the tactical methods used by Enver Hoxha. He knew very well that the Albanian partisans would be lost without the energetic support of the Yugoslav Communists. Therefore he did not hesitate to break the Mukaj pact, while at the same time accusing his *own* emissaries to the Mukaj conference —to whom he had given plenipotentiary powers—of "acting on their own authority to the prejudice of the Party's interests." In order to make absolutely certain that this humiliating, forced submission could not later be used against him, he expelled his envoys from the Party hierarchy. One of them, Gjinishi, was killed by his own comrades. The other, Dishnica, was expelled from the Party in 1946, and has never been seen since.

The annulment of the Mukaj agreement led to open conflict between the Communist-run National Freedom Movement and the other Albanian resistance movements. Hoxha's unpatriotic action could become very dangerous for him and his partisan commanders. After all, the return of the Kossovo district to Albania, as Hoxha very well knew, was universally desired by the Albanian people: A better propaganda slogan would have been hard to find. Hoxha decided to do everything possible to take the wind out of his opponents' sails. In broadsheets and proclamations to the people, he ceaselessly maintained that the National Freedom Movement was not a Communist organization, that its aim was the "liberation of Albania from slavery" and the "founding of a free and independent state," and that there was no intention of interfering with private property or private initiative in the nation's economy. He also insisted that no radical changes were envisaged, either in the social organization and customs of the people or in the organization of labor.

These hypocritical assurances and threadbare promises would not have had much chance of being believed, either by the Albanians or by the Allied observers in the country, if other events had not come to the assistance of Hoxha and his followers. The Italians quit the country in 1943. Their place, at the time the Mukaj pact was being repudiated, was taken by the Germans. The *Wehrmacht* was not interested in taking on new burdens in such a poorly developed country as Albania, so they restored a kind of independence to the Albanians. A Regency Council was put together from several pliant personalities, who dutifully proclaimed their country's neutrality. The German occupation authority's tactics of keeping out of Albanian internal affairs as much as possible caused many adherents of the National Freedom

Movement to withdraw from active political affairs. Others openly supported the Regency, either out of conviction or out of opportunism; or, often enough, because they believed that this represented the only effective obstacle to the advance of Communism. Even more decisive was the fact that the Germans' interest in Albania was conditioned by purely strategic considerations. In wide areas of the country, the military made no serious effort to exercise control, apart from guarding its own essential bases. Occupation troops mostly remained in the towns, and only occasionally sent out punitive expeditions into the mountains. As a result, large areas were left completely in the hands of the partisan groups, commanded by the National Freedom Movement. Wherever the Communists held power, the supporters of the other national resistance movements were mercilessly butchered. Those who could escape sought refuge in the towns, put themselves under German protection, and sometimes, driven by bitterness, even helped the occupation troops in their campaign against the partisans.

Nothing could have been more welcome to the Communist leaders of the National Freedom Movement, anxious as they were about their position at that time. Hoxha unleashed a violent propaganda campaign, intended to persuade both the Albanian people and the Anglo-American headquarters and supply organizations that the *Balli Kombetar* was a "fascist German front organization," whereas the National Freedom Movement was in favor of a democratic assembly which would neither be Communist-controlled nor pursue Communist objectives after the war. Hoxha's tactical plan was outlined in a secret communication sent to all the top staffs of the Communist partisan groups in September, 1943. It said that the Albanian Communists must master three propaganda theses: First, to discredit the *Balli Kombetar* in the eyes of the people by well-planned "unmasking" and tireless agitation; second, to represent the *Balli Kombetar* as the cause of the civil strife; and third, to assure the psychological preparation of the Albanian people for the fight to destroy the *Balli Kombetar*. Thus the nationalists found themselves in a hopeless position, fighting a war on two fronts. The isolation of the nationalists was only increased by the policies of Allied Headquarters, whose actions, looked at today, are very difficult to understand. Although the nationalists kept on trying to establish contact with the Allies, the Anglo-American commanders, totally misunderstanding the situation, would only help the Communists. As a result, the Communists succeeded in taking one position after another from the nationalist groups. The *Balli Kombetar* was put on the defensive, and those who escaped considered themselves lucky to be able to get out of Albania at all.

The *Legaliteti* group did not fare much better. Abas Kupi, the group's leader and a member of the Central Council of the National Freedom Movement, lost all his illusions as a result of the breaking of the Mukaj pact. Back home in the mountains, he gathered those tribal leaders who supported his movement's monarchist aims and founded his own party, the *Legaliteti* Party, at the end of 1943. He offered to conclude an alliance with the National Freedom Movement, but the Communist leaders refused. From then on, Abas Kupi was also branded as a "traitor" by the National Freedom Movement.

In spite of this, the Anglo-American liaison staffs were still anxious to win over the *Legaliteti* Party for the common resistance against the German occupation forces. In the summer of 1944, Abas Kupi, who had hitherto been sulking over the Allies' openly preferential treatment of the Communists, let himself be persuaded to order his ill-equipped men to join in the fighting. This did not cause the Germans any particular damage, but it did alarm the National Freedom Movement, which had no taste for a rival force of nationalists, armed and recognized by the Allies. Hoxha, scenting danger to himself and unwilling to take any risks, again made up his mind without hesitation. A strongly armed force of the National Freedom Movement, led by Mehmet Shehu, crossed the Shkumbini River, turned northward, and destroyed Kupi's tiny group almost to the last man. Kupi and a few followers managed to escape to Italy. Hoxha had thus succeeded in getting rid of all potential opponents within his own camp and all non-Communist competitors for the leading position in Albania, before the war in Albania was even ended.

In May, 1944, when the defeat of the German forces in the Balkans was within measurable distance, Hoxha called a conference with a view to the formation of a provisional government. On this occasion, he followed democratic usage by inviting British and American observers to the conference, as well as a strong contingent from the Yugoslav Communist Party. An "Anti-Fascist National Liberation Council" of Communists and fellow-travelers was formed. The Liberation Council constituted itself as the nation's supreme legislative and executive organ. It was also to nominate a committee which would function as the government on X-Day. A fellow-traveler was put at the head of the Liberation Council, while Hoxha made sure that he had the key position, that of Chairman of the Committee—in other words, the head of the future Government.

Hoxha's single-mindedness is further illustrated by an episode that throws a significant light on the character of the man. When the Germans had withdrawn their forces from Albania and only sporadic fighting was going on in the north, the Communist leaders took advantage of the opportunity to get rid of another of Hoxha's rivals, Lazar Fundo, who was in bad favor as a Trotskyite. Although he had been Hoxha's teacher in Paris, and had given the future dictator his first ideological lessons, he was beaten to death by his own people.

On November 29, 1944, the National Freedom Movement forces took Tirana. The Communists were in control of Albania. Hoxha had reached his goal.

What happened between the Communists' seizure of power and the moment when they had complete control of the country was identical with what happened in the other satellite countries. The backwardness and the primitive state of the country, economically and administratively, together with the Albanians' strongly developed sense of freedom, might possibly have proved a hindrance to the rapid bolshevization of the country, but this was balanced by the total lack of democratic tradition.

In the process of producing Communist conditions in their country, the Albanian Communists modeled themselves on the neighboring Yugoslav comrades. Contact between Tirana and Moscow went via Belgrade. Backed up by his Yugoslav friends, Hoxha proceeded to deal with his own countrymen in pitiless fashion. If intimidation and economic pressure failed to cow Albanians who resisted bolshevization, they were simply put to death. Stubborn opposition brought the offenders, charged with being "enemies of the people," before special courts. Albania adopted the "shortened procedure," so typical of the Soviet Union in Stalin's day, which made it possible to condemn the accused without his being heard, and excluded the possibility of appeal. A few examples from the early days of Communist rule include a group of anti-Communists in the Kukes district, another in the Kruja region, and some rebels from the area round Nahti, who were all put to death at the end of 1944. In January, 1945, eight officers of the former Albanian police were executed in Tirana, and in February, a number of "saboteurs" met the same fate in Kuchova. In April, sixty former civil servants, police officials, and members of parliament were tried and found guilty, seventeen of them condemned to be executed. So it went on, month after month and year after year, in dreadful monotony.

The breach between Tito and the Kremlin, in 1948, confronted Hoxha with the problem of whom he should choose. The Albanian Communist Party had been founded and built up during the war with Yugoslav help, and it was largely through Tito and his emissaries that Hoxha had attained his present position. Without Mugosa and Popovich, without Vukmonovic-Tempo and the other envoys from Belgrade, Hoxha and the Albanian Communists probably would never have been able to achieve their present power. After the end of hostilities, the Albanian regime had, of course, looked up to the Soviet Union as a shining example, but Albania had, in fact, become a satellite of Yugoslavia and took orders from Belgrade. In July, 1946, Hoxha and his entire cabinet had paid a visit to Belgrade, and from that time on there was no falling off in the friendship between the two countries. When Yugoslavia was expelled from the Cominform, and the campaign of mutual vilification between Moscow and Belgrade set in, the Albanian Communists were at first thrown into a state of complete confusion. They feared that the closeness of Albania's ties with Yugoslavia might tempt Moscow to excommunicate Albania too.

Hoxha, seeing a favorable opportunity to rid himself of Yugoslavia's guardianship, did not take long to reach a decision. Without batting an eyelid, he declared that he had not trusted the Yugoslavs since October, 1944. In July, 1948, the Central Committee of the Albanian Communist Party published a resolution condemning the leading Yugoslav personalities as "traitors" and "Trotskyites." In three separate passages, the resolution proclaimed Albania's solidarity with the Cominform, and the Soviet Union as the leader of the anti-imperialist camp. In order to leave no possible shadow of doubt about the finality of their break with Yugoslavia, the Albanians decided to abandon the name "Communist Party of Albania" and to call themselves the "Albanian Workers' Party."

Hoxha once more gave proof of the sureness of instinct that always enabled him to be one step ahead of his potential rivals and opponents in delicate situations. He strengthened his own position in the Party by combining with the paeans of praise of the Kremlin the removal of his most dangerous rival, Kochi Xoxe. As Dedijer's biography of Tito makes plain, the Yugoslavs had been in favor of Xoxe for some time. As a working man, he appealed to Tito far more than the educated and conceited Hoxha. Next to Hoxha, Xoxe was the most important man in the state and in the Party, having been Deputy Prime Minister, Minister of the Interior, and Chairman of the State Control Commission. Moreover, he was an old friend and comrade-in-arms of Hoxha. After the break between Belgrade and the Cominform, Xoxe condemned Tito in the same tone and with the same vehemence as the other Albanian Communists, despite the fact that he had been, if anything, slightly closer to the Yugoslavs. But it did him no good. Hoxha decided to make his rival the chief scapegoat in the course of a "purge of Titoist elements."

The way Hoxha managed this was a veritable masterpiece of Machiavellian power politics. In reforming his cabinet in October, 1948, he made Xoxe Minister for Industry. Xoxe's years of service as Minister of the Interior had given him control of the secret police, and in order to lull him into a feeling of security, Hoxha nominated Xoxe's close friend, Kerenchi, to be Minister of the Interior. This enabled Hoxha to remove a most important and dangerous weapon from Xoxe's control without causing any stir. A month later he got set to deal Xoxe the fatal blow. He relieved him of all his offices, and simultaneously deposed Xoxe's friend from his position as Minister of the Interior. All other apparent friends and

supporters of Xoxe were also fired from any key positions they held
in the state and the Party. A week later, at the First Congress of
the Albanian Communist Party in Tirana, at the beginning of November, 1948, Xoxe was given the knockout blow. Much more
would have been achieved in Albania in the postwar years, it was
proclaimed, if certain "anti-Albanian and anti-Marxist" elements
of "Yugoslav Trotskyism" had not put a spoke in the wheel. These
"elements" had been mainly controlled by Tito, but there were also
certain circles in Albania that had taken orders from him—and
Xoxe was the chief miscreant among these traitors. Xoxe was arrested the following day. In May, 1949, he was brought before a
military tribunal. During the trial, "powerful mass demonstrations"
demanded the death penalty for him. On June 11, the military
court pronounced the death sentence, which was carried out on
the same day.

But the purge did not stop there. A series of prominent Albanian
Communist leaders were also handed over to the hangman. All of
them had been charged with trying to "separate Albania from the
Soviet Union and bring the country under the influence of Belgrade."

During all this, Hoxha promoted to leading positions those
whose fortunes had been on the downgrade during the final phase
of Xoxe's police regime. Xoxe's list of those to be disposed of included Lira Belishova and Mehmet Shehu. Belishova's husband,
Nako Spiru, had committed suicide in 1947, an event which had
been made the grounds for expelling Belishova from the Central
Committee. Shehu had been relieved of his post as Chief of the
General Staff of the Albanian Army, and was expelled from the
Central Committee in 1948. Both had been under permanent surveillance by Xoxe's police, and it is pretty certain that both would
sooner or later have been put out of the way by Xoxe. Both Belishova and Shehu now rose to leading positions in the Party machine. Shehu took over Xoxe's old post as Minister of the Interior,
became Deputy Prime Minister, and was taken into the Politbureau. Since that time, he has been Hoxha's faithful vassal, having
advanced so far in the Party hierarchy that he now ranks immediately below Hoxha.

Hoxha had cold-bloodedly calculated that Moscow's patronage

would probably be less dangerous to his personal position than his loyalty to the Belgrade friends, who had once raised him on high. The essential thing now was to ensure the "unity of the cadre" with the new line. At this point, it is worth remembering that Yugoslavia had taken about as much account of Albania's national interests as the Soviets had of Yugoslavia's. One example of this was the way the Albanians had been forced to break the Mukaj pact of 1943; but this was only one of many such acts. In 1947–48, Belgrade started discussions on incorporating Albania into the Yugoslav body politic, so that when Hoxha exploited the breach between Tito and Moscow to escape the all-too-affectionate embrace of the Yugoslavs, it was by no means against his better judgment. Control by Belgrade had now been replaced by direction by Moscow. This was no less real, but it was a little less patent. Moscow was further away than Belgrade, for one thing, and there was no direct land route between the two without crossing the territory of Titoist Yugoslavia and anti-Communist Greece. There was therefore no need to fear any territorial claims by the Soviets.

Once Yugoslavia had been thrown out of the association of Communist states, Albania became the only satellite that was geographically cut off from the Eastern bloc, a fact which had certain advantages from Tirana's point of view: Drastic interference in the internal affairs of the Albanian Communists was not really possible. Hoxha could accordingly turn his attention to ensuring his grip on his own party apparatus. The erstwhile connection with the Yugoslav leaders posed an ever-present threat, and in the years that followed the Albanian Party was subjected to one purge after another.

These are only the most important examples. In 1950, a number of alleged Titoists were executed, including Abedin Shehu, the Minister of Public Works and a member of the Central Committee, together with two other members of the Central Committee, Islami and Kellezi. The charges were the same in each case; the accused had attempted to estrange Albania from the Soviet Union and to bring her under Yugoslav influence. The President of the National People's Assembly, Bekir Nou, another member of the Central Committee, was also purged. In 1952, Army General Nedship Vincani, Chief of the General Staff and a Central Committee member, was relieved of all his offices and disappeared from sight. His particular crime was that he had been a friend of Kochi Xoxe and that he had nurtured "petty-bourgeois feelings."

It need hardly be said that the purges were not confined to the top leaders of the Party. Enver Hoxha himself made this plain at the Second Party Congress of the Party in March, 1952, when he revealed that since the date of the Cominform decision to expel Yugoslavia from the socialist camp, 5,996 members and candidates had been expelled from the Albanian Party. The "unity of the cadre," Hoxha said, had now been re-established, and an important epoch in the history of the Party had thus been concluded.

True enough, there now followed a comparatively quiet period for the Party apparatus. There was no subsequent purge until 1955, when two prominent Party members, Tuk Jakova and Berri Spahiu, both of whom had been on the way out for some time, were expelled and arrested. After 1948, Jakova had been, in turn, President of the Trade Unions, Chairman of the National Assembly, Deputy Prime Minister, Minister for Industry, and Ambassador in Yugoslavia and Hungary. He played a prominent part in the campaign against Xoxe, and after Xoxe's liquidation he climbed to the highest rungs of the Party ladder, having become Second Secretary of the Central Committee and a member of the Politbureau. But by 1951, he was already on the way down. He lost his seat in the Politbureau, and in 1952 Hoxha charged him with "right deviationism and disobedience of Party orders in religious matters" (Jakova had been a Roman Catholic). However, the final blow did not fall until 1955, when he lost all his offices and was arrested. It is rumored that he later died in jail.

Major-General Bedri Spahiu had made his name in 1945, as public prosecutor in the trials of war criminals and enemies of the people before a Special Court. He remained true to the Party line throughout all the purges. Before he himself fell a victim to Hoxha's policies, he was head of the Agitation and Propaganda Section of the Party organization, President of the Soviet-Albanian Friendship Society, Deputy Prime Minister, and Minister for Culture and Education.

The removal of Jakova and Spahiu was not entirely unexpected; the shadow was cast as early as 1951. It must therefore be assumed that the reasons for their decline and fall were not directly political. It looked as though the real reason was that neither of them was really capable of fulfilling the tasks of leadership that they had been given to do. It was not until later that the Albanian propaganda machine came out with the claim that these two had been in contact with the Yugoslavs.

After the purges, there was no longer any opposition in existence, and the cadres had been brought sharply into line with the dictator's policies. This reduction of the cadres to total subservience was to prove most useful a short time later, when Hoxha was again faced with a perilous trial of strength. In May, 1955, Khrushchev and Bulganin arrived in Belgrade to try to patch things up with Tito. The Soviet leaders exerted themselves to represent the past seven years of hate and slander as a "misunderstanding," for which, they said, the "traitor Beria" must bear the entire blame. This meeting in Belgrade caused confusion and uneasiness in Tirana, as did the breach between Moscow and Belgrade in 1948. But Hoxha, with his usual slick reaction, soon swung over to the Moscow line. The Albanian anti-Yugoslav campaign was called off. *Pravda* published an article written by Hoxha, pointing out that misunderstandings did sometimes arise between brothers, but that sooner or later they were bound to be cleared up. In September, Hoxha made a speech in which he recalled the brotherhood-in-arms of the Albanian and Yugoslav partisans and emphasized the solidarity between the fraternal parties. The "unfortunate happenings" had been simply and solely due to those "imperialist agents and enemies of socialism, Beria and Abakumov."

But on one point Hoxha remained adamant. While other East European countries were rehabilitating prominent Party leaders who had been put to death in 1948 for allegedly conspiring with Titoists, Hoxha saw to it that nothing was done to rehabilitate Xoxe, his former arch-rival, who had, of course, been executed on precisely the same charge. This particular point in time, when Moscow and Belgrade were getting ready to make up and be friends, seemed to Hoxha to be just the wrong time for doing the proper thing by Xoxe, since that might well have entailed having to do penance to Belgrade, too, a proceeding that could have endangered the political stability of Albania. Hoxha reasoned that

Xoxe must remain Albanian Public Enemy No. 1, which he is to this very day. If you talk to Albanian Party functionaries about Xoxe, you will always receive the same answer—if an Albanian court has declared a man a traitor, then you can take it that he was.

Every trace of Kochi Xoxe's memory was erased in true Stalinist fashion. In the War Museum in Tirana, I saw a painting depicting the entry of the partisan leaders into Tirana after the country's liberation. I had previously seen a photograph of this scene, and I remembered that marching to the right of Hoxha was his friend, Kochi Xoxe. In the painting I saw, however, all trace of his image had been carefully painted out.

A few months after the meeting in Belgrade, the Twentieth Party Congress of the Soviet Communist Party brought the Albanian Party leaders a new and highly unpleasant surprise. It was only with a good deal of hesitation and misgiving that Hoxha brought himself to toe the line of Soviet reformism. He easily sidestepped the question of the "cult of personality," the central topic of discussion at the Twentieth Party Congress, by simply declaring that the cult of personality had not existed in Albania since 1954—that is, long before the Congress. The Albanian leaders did initiate a limited number of destalinization measures and the principle of collective leadership was formally introduced. The police were slightly cut down, internal Party criticism allowed, the so-called Democratic Front dusted off, and some promises made in regard to the supply of consumer goods. But that was all.

Yugoslav sources now say that at this time there was a good deal of dissatisfaction in Tirana with the leadership of Hoxha and Mehmet Shehu. Several delegates to the Third Party Congress in Tirana in May, 1956, are reported to have demanded discussion of the Twentieth Soviet Party Congress, the cult of personality, the Xoxe affair, relations with Yugoslavia, the standard of living, and democracy within the Party. But these Yugoslav reports must be treated with reservation. It is possible that a few Albanian comrades were flirting with Yugoslav revisionism, but, on the other hand, their previous experience with Hoxha's regime makes it unlikely that these Party members would have put these points up for public discussion. They would have been too afraid of the merciless dictator. Furthermore, the Party machine had been brought firmly into line and every apparent or potential opponent put out of the way after the break with Yugoslavia. If Hoxha had sensed the slightest deviation from his own views in the critical months of 1956, he would certainly have moved to crush it, fast and mercilessly. As it was, nothing changed and the Albanian Party was spared any more drastic purges for years to come. Even when the outbreak of the Hungarian revolt appeared to confirm the theories of Hoxha and his lieutenants, the dictator saw no reason to purge the Party again. In November, 1956, the Albanian propaganda authorities made it known, as a reminder and a warning, that in the late 1940's prominent Communists like Lira Gega and her husband Dali Ndren, both members of the Albanian Central Committee, together with the Yugoslav Peter Bulatovic, had been shot for maintaining contact with the "security service of a foreign power"—obviously that of Yugoslavia. But these were old cases. No new charges were made, a sure sign that Hoxha was satisfied with the morale inside the Party.

Hoxha did not fail to make propaganda use of his victory, however, triumphantly pointing out where premature destalinization might also have led Albania. He acquitted the Hungarian Stalinists Rakosi and Gerö "of all blame for the Hungarian rising." The incidents in Poznan he called "nothing but provocation by reactionary and right-opportunist elements," which, under the pretext of fighting the Stalin cult, "had endangered socialism in East Europe." In saying this, Hoxha was giving notice that he regarded the destalinization proclaimed after the Twentieth Party Congress as an extremely dangerous softening of the general Communist line. The modified Communism *à la* Khrushchev, if it were to be transfered to Albania, would inevitably mean a dangerous undermining of Hoxha's position; and might one day even cost him his head.

There was no sign of disquiet in the Albanian Party. Khrushchev's dithering *vis-à-vis* Yugoslavia had deprived him of even the possibility of interfering with it. Hoxha's position and policies did not seem endangered again until Hoxha was faced with his third trial of strength.

The year 1960 seemed to present a favorable opportunity to draw the logical political conclusions from Albania's steadily in-

creasing mistrust of Moscow. There can be no doubt that when
the possibility of a change of course was being discussed, a number of voices uttered objections to the idea of abandoning Soviet
protection and patronage. Again Hoxha showed himself determined to act quickly. For the first time in years, there was a purge
which took care of the undecided elements in the Party. Lira
Belishova and Kocho Tashko, as has already been related, were
expelled from the Party for "serious errors and hostile activities"—
which meant in fact that they had had doubts about taking an
anti-Moscow course and feared its concrete effects. However,
there were no more purges after that. With surprising speed,
Hoxha managed to restore the "unity of the cadre" in consonance
with his own ideas. Albanian functionaries assured me that in
contrast to other sections of the people, who were uneasy about
the change of course, the cadre had been firmly united behind
Hoxha.

That Enver Hoxha has been laying down the Albanian Party
line for more than twenty years is due to the indisputable fact
that he has never had the slightest scruple about the methods he
has had to use to preserve his position and authority. This can be
seen from the examination of the Party's top men. Of the members
of the original provisional Central Committee of 1941, only one is
still in his post—Hoxha. Of the first properly constituted Central
Committee of the Albanian Communist Party of 1943, there is
also only one member left—Hoxha. Of the thirty-one members of
the second Central Committee, elected in 1944, only nine are still
in post—provided that some of them have not recently been fired
without the fact becoming public.

While I was in Tirana I was able to see for myself how well
public institutions are prepared for any eventuality arising from
the dictator's changes of heart. As in every museum in Albania,
the visitor to the Tirana War Museum sees photographic portraits
of the members of the Politbureau looking down on him from the
walls. But in order to allow the governor of the museum to cope
with any change in the political scene, the pictures can be removed from their frames. The gallery of the Albanian Communist
nobility can be brought up to date in a matter of minutes. The
degree to which the photographs have faded provides the visitor

with a sure indication of the length of time the subjects have basked in the favor of the dictator.

Enver Hoxha has often been compared with his great model, Joseph Stalin. This comparison may be justified up to a point—for example, with respect to their common instinctive feel for power, or to their ability to eliminate cold-bloodedly any obstacles in their path. Hoxha has also proven himself to be a master in the art of weighing the risks. There is, of course, a difference in the amount of education of the two men, but history has shown that intelligence and education are no bar to the possessor's willingness to use terrorism. Without question, this facet of Hoxha's character has had a direct influence on the politics of his country.

IV

Albania and the Sino-Soviet Dispute

PREVIOUS CHAPTERS HAVE covered the reasons behind the growth of the Albanian Communists' mistrust of the Soviet leaders over the years. The destalinization measures in the satellites, the Soviet attempts at reconciliation with Tito, and the Kremlin's foreign-policy maneuvers in the Balkans seemed to run counter to Albanian interests and to the country's internal political structure. Hoxha's cold intelligence left him under no illusion about the pressures that the fine meshing of complex causes and effects might put him under. He foresaw still graver difficulties to come.

Hoxha also saw that there was nothing he could do about the Soviet's new policies. The Albanian Communist leaders could take no action except to keep an anxious watch on the course of events. Politically, Albania is a lightweight. Her economic resources are far too meager to be a bait to the affluent Soviet patron—indeed, Albania's economic dependence on the grace and favor of the other Eastern-bloc countries has already been observed. Even the value of her geographical position, which might otherwise have aroused Soviet interest from the long-term strategic point of view, has been reduced to a minimum by the advent of the rocket as a weapon. Besides, the country is both too small and too exposed for the kind of strategic planning undertaken by the General Staff planners, who think in terms of vast areas.

It looked as though Hoxha and his Party had no alternative but to follow the course being taken by the Soviets and their satellites. Moscow's favor could not be cast away lightly. Criticism, if it were to be exercised at all, must be hinted at and nothing more (not that there was much chance that it would produce any noticeable effect). Defiance or reproach would simply have increased the likelihood that Moscow's general policy line would be followed without any regard for the Albanian nation and Party interests.

It was in this setting that the signs of an unexpected and welcome change appeared. The first hint was the leaking out of the news of a controversy between Moscow and Peking. Just as the breach between Tito and Stalin had given Hoxha the opportunity to rid himself of the oppressive weight of Yugoslav protection, so this new turn of events offered him another chance to change partners, and thus sidestep the ominous fate that Moscow's policies seemed to be preparing for Albania. At almost the same moment that the quarrel between the Russian and the Chinese Communists flared up before the eyes of the world, the Albanian leaders made known their change of political course.

It is tempting to think it was mainly tactical considerations that persuaded Hoxha to make his change-over; and there is no doubt that any Communist partner would have been welcome to Hoxha, as long as it fulfilled certain essential conditions. These conditions included hostility to Yugoslavia, and a negative attitude to the pragmatic pseudo-revisionism that the Kremlin had been working toward in the past few years. It is precisely this latter point that deprives the strange alliance between the mighty Far Eastern partner and the tiny, insignificant satellite on the Adriatic of any fortuitous character. Quite apart from tactical considerations, the alliance is based on an identity of interests with a strong ideological flavor. In spite of the radical differences between the two countries that make their partnership such an extraordinary one, there are certain common factors, such as their parallel views on the use of power and on the tactics Communists should use in dealing with the hostile, non-Communist world. Some of the arguments brought forward by the Chinese in their dispute with the Soviets must have been received with enthusiastic agreement in Tirana, since they closely corresponded with the views Albania held in relation to the tension between herself and the U.S.S.R. It will be necessary to look at the main points of difference between Moscow and Peking in order to bring out the factors that make Albania's shift of allegiance more than a purely tactical maneuver.

In the preceding years, Peking had developed three theses which stood in contradiction to the Kremlin's policy line. They concerned Communist internal policy, specifically, how the implementation of a theory can best and most speedily be achieved; the attitude toward the West; and Communist activities in the underdeveloped countries. The fact that all three of these questions are purely tactical ones does not diminish their importance; they must not be underrated. It is just such differences of opinion about the methods Communists should use in their actual work that can so easily lead to serious and lasting conflicts between the Communist parties.

The Clocks of Peking Show a Different Time

It is always a delicate business to undertake a comparative analysis of two nations, whose leaders, while they support the same principles and pursue the same objectives, spring from peoples with totally different histories and traditions. It is doubly difficult in the intellectual sphere, which defies exact assessment. Neither in Russia nor in China can Communism as a concept be considered in isolation from the spiritual and cultural traditions of the country itself. The years of the two revolutions, 1917 in Russia and 1949 in China, represent no absolute break with what had become organic to these countries in past centuries. Thus it will always remain a moot point as to how much of Soviet bolshevism is Communist and how much is purely Russian; and, similarly, how much of Maoism is primarily Chinese and how much is Marxist. Whatever the answer may be, the fact remains that the amalgamation of a revolutionary, modern, utopian philosophy with the spiritual heritage of the past has created a certain attitude of mind or political consciousness in the Communist élite that is necessarily different for each of the two centers of Communist power.

However, even if we disregard these important factors, and take as a starting point a hypothetical equivalence of intellectual and revolutionary view between Moscow and Peking, there are other reasons which would lead to disparities in the ideological and intellectual sphere. For example, the difference in the stages of development reached by the two countries cannot be ignored. Differing degrees of maturity automatically create variations in the internal dynamics of different countries. This was particularly well illustrated by a similar situation that had developed shortly after World War II. In his book on Tito, Dedijer describes how Stalin ordered the Chinese comrades to Moscow so that he could tell them that in the opinion of the Kremlin, a Communist rising in China stood no chance of succeeding. Mao, he said, should find a *modus vivendi* with Chiang Kai-shek, cooperate in forming a government with him, and disband the revolutionary forces. The Chinese representatives gave every appearance of accepting this advice while they were in Moscow, but once they were back home they did the exact opposite. The success of Mao's revolution proved them right. It is therefore understandable that Peking, even after the Communists seized power, had no great opinion of Moscow's tactical ideas and preferred to trust to themselves in developing their policies.

Not that the Chinese had much muscle to flex. Their country was in a poor state and needed the Soviet Union's help. The example of Yugoslavia had made clear to all the Communist states just what they could expect if they were so foolhardy as to rebel against Stalin. Moreover, Stalin's policies on the use of power contained nothing the Chinese could actually object to, so they scrupulously followed the general line laid down by Moscow—without, however, allowing this to affect their own increased confidence in themselves.

It was not until Stalin died, and the Soviet Union itself went into a transitional stage, that there appeared the first signs of views contrary to those of Moscow and peculiar to the Chinese. This new development made itself particularly evident at the Twentieth Soviet Party Congress, at which the first attacks on Stalin were made. At the beginning, the Chinese delegates made no comment on the Kremlin's new line. Later, having weighed all the risks, they put out a carefully calculated statement which contained an evaluation of Stalin that was quite different from Moscow's, and that consequently rejected the new line ordered by the Soviet Party leaders.

The events in Poland in October, 1956, provided a new opportunity for Peking to publicize its own ideas. For the first time in their history, the Chinese Communists actively intervened in East European affairs, putting out political declarations and openly supporting the efforts of the new Polish leaders to loosen the bonds that held them tied to the Soviet Union. They warned Moscow against "great power chauvinism," which, they said, contradicted the principles of "proletarian internationalism." The support Poland was given by the Chinese at that time has often been wrongly interpreted in the West, where many at first thought the Chinese were also supporting a "more liberal and enlightened" form of bolshevism. The Chinese did, in fact, favor extensive internal political autonomy, but still only on condition that overall control was maintained by the Party. A simplified statement of the Chinese position would be that in analyzing the events in Poland, the Chinese felt that Gomulka's Poland would become more Polish but at the same time more Communist. When it turned out that Poland, while becoming more Polish, threatened to become "more Western," Mao left no doubt about his disapproval.

The result of the Hungarian revolt increased China's unwillingness to face the risks involved in supporting any tendencies to independence. In December, 1956, the Chinese Central Committee drew the necessary conclusions in an analysis of the European insurrections. While the validity of the formula "individual roads to socialism" was confirmed and emphasized, the real stress was on "the dictatorship of the proletariat," which was declared to be the most important principle of Marxism.

In the summer of 1958, the Chinese Communist rulers indicated that they had not ceased to question the Soviet Union's claim as the only true interpretor of Communist teaching. Peking introduced the People's Communes, an organization that made much greater demands on the life of the individual than any social institution in the Soviet Union. The Communes became cells in the structure of the Chinese state and Party. They were of enormous extent, embracing many villages. Each Commune contained, as a rule, 25,000 people, and sometimes as many as 300,000. The collectives, which had become the regular form of agricultural organization in the Soviet Union, had also been steadily increasing in size over the years, but they had never assumed the proportions of the Chinese Communes. Moreover, unlike the Soviet collectives, the Chinese Communes embraced every sector of the lives of their members.

The challenge of the People's Communes to the Soviet Union was not so much their economic or organizational significance, but the Chinese claim that the concept of the Communes represented an important contribution to Marxism-Leninism—a claim which gave the measure ideological significance. The Chinese Party theoretician, Chen Po-ta, declared that Mao's inspired plan meant that in China the transition from socialism to Communism was already beginning. The resolution by the Central Committee on the setting up of the Communes contained the statement that the realization of Communism in China was no longer something for the distant future. Collective ownership of the People's Communes already contained elements of total public ownership, and the final transition to the ardently desired target of complete Communism would only take three to six years.

The claim of being able to build up Communism in a few years by introducing a particular organizational form of communal living was in direct contradiction to Soviet teaching on the graduated nature of the road to the last stage of Communism. The Soviet ideological experts had long been preaching that "the basis of socialism" must first be established. According to a decision by the Soviet Party, this phase came to an end in the Soviet Union in 1932, that is, fifteen years after the revolution; and it was only then that a start could be made on setting up "the socialist social system." This was "substantially" achieved by 1939. In 1952, the building up of the socialist society was regarded as having been "achieved," and a beginning could then be made on the transition to Communism, the "basis" of which would be established after the current Five Year Plan, in 1965. The Chinese, on the other hand, with barely seven years of "socialist construction" behind them, were claiming not only that they would complete the building-up of socialism in the shortest possible time, thanks to their universal elixir called "People's Communes," but, worse still, that they would complete "the main part" of the building up of Communism in a few years.

The challenge implied in the Communes was made all the more serious by the concomitant adulation accorded to Mao and his ideas. Liu Lan-tao, a member of the Secretariat of the Chinese Central Committee, proclaimed that Comrade Mao was "the most

outstanding revolutionary, statesman, and Marxist-Leninist theoretician of the age." The Party Secretary, Wang En Mao, went
even further, claiming that the scale by which an individual would
be adjudged a genuine Marxist was his understanding of Mao
Tse-tung's ideology.

While such hymns of praise to the Chinese dictator were clearly
intended for home consumption, they nevertheless contained an
assertion that was bound to be noticed far beyond the borders of
China. It was not by chance that when the plan to establish the
People's Communes was first made public, Chen Po-ta quoted the
father of the Russian Revolution, Lenin, who had pointed out
that in Asia there were special conditions which were unknown
to the European nations and demanded special methods. The im-
plication of this was that the concept of the People's Communes
furnished an alternative to the Soviet road, an alternative which
above all should serve as a guide to the peoples of the underdeveloped countries.

It took a long time for Moscow to come up with a clear and
considered reply to this Chinese move, presumably because it had
taken the Soviets so completely by surprise. In June, 1958, Khrushchev had still been praising the Chinese comrades for their "use
of Leninist methods" in the building up of an agricultural co-
operative system. In August, a few days before the resolution on
the setting up of the People's Communes was announced to the
world, a *Pravda* leading article had hailed the "enthusiasm" of the
Chinese peasants for the "great possibilities" of the cooperatives.
Experimental Communes had already been started in the spring
of 1958, and were, in some cases, already completed when the
intention to introduce the Commune system was made known in
September.

Initially, the Soviet propaganda machine noticeably played
down the new development, and the people of the Soviet Union
were not allowed to learn very much about the existence of this
new form of socialist economy. The political and economic problems created by Peking's go-it-alone move remained concealed
from them. What the Soviet leaders thought about the Chinese
experiment was made known by Khrushchev in conversations he
had with Senator Humphrey of the United States, and by Mikoyan

in interviews during his visit to America. Khrushchev called the Commune experiment "old-fashioned and retrograde." Six months later, at a meeting in Poznan, he told his audience what a failure the Soviet Commune experiment had been in the early years of bolshevist rule in Russia.

While Soviet propaganda did not actually openly disavow it, the Chinese experiment appears to have been intensively discussed in Party circles. There was a direct connection between the setting up of the People's Communes in China and the summoning of the extraordinary Twenty-First Soviet Party Congress. The Soviet leaders doubtless wanted to announce their theses on the "true" road to Communism as an alternative to the Chinese ideas. There seem also to have been bilateral efforts to bridge the gap that had opened up in the theory on this central point of Communist ideology. In October, 1958, one of the most prominent Soviet ideologists, Stepanyan, had still been suggesting that differing degrees of development made it necessary to distinguish between a European and an Asiatic group of socialist countries. The European socialist countries, because of their superiority in the technical field, would reach the final goal of Communism before the Asiatic group. However, at the Twenty-First Party Congress, Khrushchev unexpectedly dropped this idea, and maintained that all the countries of the Eastern bloc would pass into the advanced stage of Communism "more or less simultaneously," a difference which made it clear that the Kremlin leaders were doing their best to avoid aggravating the dispute between them and Peking.

On their side, the Chinese had obviously given way to Soviet insistence to some extent. In December, 1958, a decision of the Chinese Central Committee removed some of the more radical points from the Commune concept. Following the example of Stalin, who had put a stop to the cruelties of the collectivization program in 1930 on the grounds that success had "gone to the head" of many cadres, the Chinese, repeating this formulation word for word, warned against overhasty development. At the same time, the Chinese extended the period required for the transition to Communism from six years to twenty. In principle, however, the pattern of the People's Communes remained as it had been, and it was probably this fact that made Khrushchev take a swing at the Chinese comrades in his speech at the Twenty-First Party Congress. It was impossible, he said, not to be critical of those Communists who wanted to realize Communism "at far too great a speed." His disparaging remarks on "out-of-date" experiments from the period of Soviet "war Communism," and the dangers of an "equalization of distribution based on the number of mouths," left no doubt whom he meant.

To this very day the Soviets have fought shy of any more detailed discussion of the Chinese Commune experiment. However, it is still part of the ideological arsenal of the Chinese, who thus keep up their claim to have a special road to Communism as an alternative to the example set by the Soviets. The Communist elite of the world was reminded of this claim when Mao accelerated the formation of the People's Communes in the towns in April, 1960. The Soviets did not go into this any more closely either.

While there can be no question about the ideological importance of the Commune concept for international Communism, it is equally certain that there were other factors that played a part in the plan to establish the Communes, although we do not know which of them was paramount. One of them was the economic factor. In the spring of 1958, the Chinese Communists had started an economic program under the slogan "the great leap forward," a program which demanded almost superhuman efforts from the people. The central problem facing the Party was how to deal with the catastrophic lack of capital needed to support the projected industrialization of the country. This lack of means became all the more pressing as Soviet sources of supply gradually began to dry up. The only solution seemed to be a massive drive to build up a primitive industry in the agricultural areas, with the abundant supply of labor going a long way to make up for the lack of capital. A quasimilitary organization on the agricultural level under vigorous and uniform command would boost the rate of development, the intention being to transform China into an industrial country in the shortest possible time and simultaneously to fulfill the needs of the rapidly increasing population.

Here, too, the Soviets had a cautionary word to say. As far back as 1934, Stalin had pointed out that the failure of Soviet Communes founded after the Revolution had been due to insufficient technical know-how, lack of raw materials, and the premature attempt to bring everyone down to the same level. Stalin's words were still very much in the mind of his successors. Khrushchev told Senator Humphrey that the founders of the first Communes in the Soviet Union had understood "little of Communism and of the way it should be built up." The Soviet economists and ideologists had repeatedly made it clear, long before the Chinese founded their People's Communes, that the aims of Communism could only be attained on the basis of superabundance and highly developed technical facilities.

Apart from the ideological and economic reasons, there was a third reason that induced the Chinese to bring in the Communes: This was the political necessity to subordinate the enormous mass of the people to a more strongly disciplined organization. At the beginning of 1957, Mao had decided to introduce a movement that will be known in history as "Let a Hundred Flowers Bloom," whereby the Party cadres were to be allowed greater freedom of speech and the functionaries were instructed to allow criticism. In the ensuing Cheng Feng campaign, which was to serve "to correct the mode of working," even non-Party members were encouraged to criticize the Party and its policies.

Understandably enough, the people hesitated to make use of their freedom. They had not forgotten the years of terror, and the fear of reprisals kept them silent. However, the leading functionaries continued to assure them that from now on they could talk freely. The result was that by May, 1957, the floodgates had opened and a torrent of criticism and bitter reproach poured out, flooding the Party with hitherto pent-up anger and discontent. The cadres were accused of arrogance, the greed of the functionaries for material privileges was attacked, their contempt for the law laid bare, and their outrageous interference in scientific work and economic affairs assailed. The most courageous of the critics went so far as to claim that the worst features of the regime were not due to abuse of power merely by individual officials, but also by the top Party leaders—or even that they were the result of the system called "proletarian dictatorship." It was not long before the original fears of the critics were realized. The Government changed its attitude sooner than anyone expected. In June, the Peking "People's Paper" began a campaign against "right-wing deviationists" and hurled about charges of "counterrevolutionary plotting." Mass arrests began and, by July, the reign of terror was once more in full swing.

Many people in the West have wondered whether the "Hundred Flowers and Cheng Feng" campaign was a devilish maneuver by the Party leaders to smoke out the hidden opponents of the regime; or whether the leaders at first acted in good faith, only to be shocked by the revelation of the extent of the hatred people felt for the Communist regime and by the amount of resistance to it. There is much to support the first theory. After the attack on the "right-wing deviationists and counterrevolutionaries," some highly placed Party officials made it known that the purpose had merely been to lure the victims into the trap in order to protect the "proletarian dictatorship." And is it conceivable that the events in Poland and Hungary six months previously had not warned Peking what might happen if the people were given more freedom?

It has not yet been possible to fathom the motives behind the "Hundred Flowers" period, but one thing is clear: The Communists were a long way from being as firmly in the saddle as the Party thought necessary, nor were its theories and authority as respected by all—especially by the intellectuals—as they ought to have been. This experience may have made a considerable contribution to the idea of introducing the People's Communes. At all events, less than a year after the wilting of the "Hundred Flowers," the introduction of the Communes began. Their introduction made it easier to put into practice the maxims that have become typical of Chinese Communism. The practice of total regimentation brings every living soul into the community, and offers a perfect opportunity to indoctrinate the individual in the Party's ideas. At the head of the Communes are the cadres, which are utterly devoted to the Party and which can make use of their position to cement the Party's absolute authority. No other system would offer the Party agitators the same opportunity of hammering ideological maxims into the people so unceasingly and intensively, or of forming their thoughts in every aspect of their lives. Total organization, total authority, and total ideology—these are the three pillars on which the Chinese Communist system rests.

It may be argued that the Chinese system is not fundamentally different from the system in the other Communist countries. There is this difference: China is going all out to increase the degree of totalitarianism, for she believes that the complete form of totalitarianism is essential if the government is to overcome the difficulties facing it. In the Soviet Union and the satellites, on the other hand, some attempt at least is being made to find a new and milder form of the totalitarian system. The Chinese are still in their Stalinist phase, not only for historical and ideological reasons, but also for reasons of political expediency. This Stalinist stage is evident not only in the externals but also, and even more so, in the unremitting fear of crisis that overtakes every totalitarian regime before overhasty political, social, and economic development has settled down into a condition which can serve as a transition to a quieter, more stable era.

Peaceful Coexistence—Two Points of View

As 1960 began, the difference of opinion between the Soviets and the Chinese on the Communes faded into the background, and attention henceforth centered on another question which attracted world-wide attention because of its possible effects on the East-West conflict. The focus of dispute shifted to the interpretation of a central point in Marxist-Leninist foreign-policy theory, namely, the limits and content of the Soviet pattern for peaceful coexistence.

In 1956, at the Twentieth Party Congress, Khrushchev had announced a formula which, as the policy of "peaceful coexistence," was to be the general line for the Soviet Communist Party. The present time, he said, was characterized by two factors. First, there were now available weapons with a hitherto undreamed-of destructive power. Second, the socialist camp had become such a power group that the capitalists could at least be stopped from unleashing war. He indicated the importance of the neutral countries, which, together with the socialist camp, formed a gigantic "peace zone" that would force the "vultures of the imperialist world" to capitulate. This situation meant that a balance of forces was now ensured, which, in turn, provided Communism with new opportunities to advance its frontiers. These premises provided the Soviet leaders with the basis for rethinking their foreign policy. The Kremlin abandoned the theses of the inevitability of wars in the imperialist era of human development, and shifted the emphasis to the possibility of seizing power by peaceful means.

These reformulations did not imply any renouncing of the use of military force or any denial of the necessity for revolutions. As Khrushchev told the Twentieth Party Congress, there were occasions when the use of force in the form of war would be completely justified. Intervention, he said, was still an admissible political action; and he gave as examples the occupation of the Baltic States in 1940, and the Prague *Putsch* in 1948. Nevertheless, the emphasis was now on the possibility of achieving the transition to Communism by peaceful means. In the Kremlin's view, the equalizing of the atomic balance of power and the growing strength of the socialist camp provided a basis on which smart political and diplomatic maneuvering could not only neutralize or remove the West's strategic positions, but also furnish openings for Communist penetration. Intelligent employment of the East bloc's military and economic strength could force the capitalist states to realize that certain positions had become untenable. Provided they could do it without losing face, they would then be perfectly prepared to relinquish those positions.

This reshaping of the Soviets' foreign-policy strategy also gave rise to changes in the tactics to be used against the West. It must be made to look as though the menacing revolutionary impetus had been slowed down. The Communists' readiness to engage in political end economic (though not ideological) competition must be made plain. Moscow must show that you could talk to the Russians and that the differences between East and West could be resolved by negotiation. This was Moscow's line at all levels, from the diplomatic to the summit.

At first, Peking loyally followed the new course set by the Soviet comrades. Mao obviously thought that Moscow's attitude was a propaganda maneuver which, in the field of practical politics, would produce only profit for the East. Friction did not arise until Mao began to get the impression that what the Kremlin was doing involved not merely peace propaganda, but serious peace diplomacy. This happened in the summer of 1958, during the Middle East crisis.

When United States troops landed in Lebanon, and it looked as if the revolution in Iraq that the Communists had welcomed so enthusiastically might be nullified, Khrushchev demanded a summit conference at which the three Western Powers, the Soviet Union, and India could discuss Middle East problems. When the Western Powers suggested holding this conference in the U.N. Security Council, Khrushchev at first seemed inclined to agree. But then events took an unexpected turn. Khrushchev flew to Peking very suddenly, spent a few days there in negotiation—and thereafter there was no further mention of a summit conference. There is little doubt that Moscow gave up the idea as the result of urgent pressure by Peking. It is clear that Khrushchev had not only busied himself in Asiatic affairs without consulting his Chinese allies, he had also suggested a meeting in which India, China's "arch-rival," was to participate; and to top it all, he had been prepared to agree to negotiations in the United Nations Security Council, with Chiang Kai-shek, Peking's "arch-enemy," taking part.

In 1959, there was more friction between the two Communist centers, when Moscow began making efforts to bring about talks with the United States. Peking had no objection to this at first, and the trips by Mikoyan, Kozlov, and Khrushchev caused the Chinese no great anxiety. But when the Camp David conversations seemed to presage a relaxation of tension apparently confined to relations between the West and the Soviet Union, Mao decided to act. He was afraid that any agreement between the two greatest powers on earth would result in the lessening of the chances that Chinese demands would be fulfilled. Any reconciliation between Moscow and the West would prejudice Chinese interests, as long as Red China was not included in the conversation and negotiations. The Soviets had grown too powerful and self-assured to be talked into changing their plans. However, the ideological arena seemed to offer a chance to get results, since it was there that Mao and his men felt themselves on sure ground.

The Soviet leaders had based their new foreign-policy line on certain theses by Lenin. Lenin had not been hostile to the idea of peaceful coexistence. As far back as 1920, he had supported the "peaceful coexistence" of peoples and states having differing social systems. However, in contrast to the present-day Soviets, and just like Stalin after him, Lenin had regarded peaceful coexistence as nothing but a temporary cessation of hostilities which would enable the Communists to improve their own position and gather strength for the final thrust. Lenin always believed in the inevitability of wars between the two camps, just as Stalin did; and both of them attached considerable importance to civil war as a stage in the spreading of Communism. Any negotiations with the enemies of the "proletarian vanguard" must be thought of merely as a tactical measure undertaken to gain a breather, and not intended to conclude permanent peace with the enemy.

On September 16, 1959, the day following Khrushchev's arrival in the United States, the Chinese Communist mouthpiece *Red Flag* attacked the Soviet leader, warning against any illusions about the real nature of imperialism. It was a mistake to think that imperialism could change its face; and it was equally mistaken to believe that one should avoid provoking the imperialists. Provocation was not a word that had any application in the case of the "imperialist jackals." Khrushchev was not impressed. Both during his stay in the United States and in the course of his subsequent visit to Peking, he testified to his belief in the earnestness of the American Government's desire for a relaxation of international tension. He called on his audience in Peking to regard coexistence as a real possibility; there was no other way.

Khrushchev's warning was not well received in Peking, and the Chinese continued to sneer at the Soviet foreign-policy tactics. The question whether wars were inevitable or not began to play an ever-increasing part in the argument. At the Hungarian Communist Party Conference in December, 1959, Khrushchev was forced to come right out and say that no Communist Party "that really regarded itself as Communist" had ever "set its hopes on achieving its aims by means of war." The Chinese reply to this, given on the occasion of Stalin's birthday, consisted of a series of quotations from the classical Bolshevist authorities on the immutable character of imperialism, and thus, in logical consequence, on the inevitability of wars.

In February, 1960, the Warsaw Pact states met in Moscow. Officially, only agricultural affairs were supposed to be on the agenda, but the fact that prominent Party leaders took part and the text of the closing communique made it clear that much more important matters than agriculture had been discussed. The outcome of the conference was contained in the thesis that as a result of "the growing power of the peace forces," the world would now enter a period of negotiations designed to resolve the most important matters of international contention. This was decisively rejected by Kang Sheng, the observer Red China had sent to the conference (although China was not a member of the Warsaw Pact). In his view, the imperialists had not altered their aggressive character one iota, and all the West's alleged "readiness to talk peace" was nothing more than a gesture without any genuine desire for peace behind it. To make China's standpoint absolutely clear, Kang Sheng declared, "No international disarmament agreement or other international agreement is binding on China without the participation and the signature of the Chinese People's Republic." Neither the Soviet nor the satellite press published Sheng's remarks. Only the Chinese papers gave prominence to them, and that they did with a will.

Shortly after this meeting, the real attack began. The Chinese took advantage of the ceremonies held to mark the ninetieth anniversary of Lenin's birth to attack the Soviet thesis that wars were not inevitable. While the Chinese agreed with their Soviet comrades that it was theoretically possible to avoid war in the present epoch, the Chinese ideologists regarded this possibility as much less likely to be realized than Moscow would admit. As long as the imperialist system remained alive, they said, war—the epitome of force—would not be done away with. It was still an inevitable corollary of the system of exploitation; and the imperialistic system was the source of all wars in modern times. The Marxist-Leninists, they added, must never sink into the slough of bourgeois pacifism: not even the possibility of a world-wide atomic war must make them waver.

The Chinese were obviously less worried about the risk of an atomic war than their Soviet comrades. Certainly, they argued, every effort should be made to prevent the terrible suffering a war would bring upon humanity, but Moscow was exaggerating the dangers. This kind of overstatement would inevitably result in the weakening of resistance to imperialism and the creation of an extremely dangerous degree of circumspection. At the sight of such a "ferocious beast as war," it would be fatal to display "the slightest sign of cowardice." And finally, if the imperialists were to be so foolhardy as to unleash an atomic war, then the result would be what had already been demonstrated by the Russian and Chinese revolutions after the First and Second World Wars —the people would be "compensated for their suffering." On the ruins of dead imperialism, the victorious peoples would build a civilization that would stand a thousand times higher than the capitalist system, and a truly wonderful future would be in sight.

This challenge was answered by one of the most prominent Communists, Otto Kuusinen. He did not deny the aggressive character of imperialism, but maintained that it was not sufficient to go on repeating this truism. Instead, the task before them was to save mankind from being plunged into catastrophe by aggressive imperialism. The ratio of forces had shifted to such an extent, he said, that the transition to socialism could be completed in stages, without the people having to pay the enormous price of war. Lenin himself had foreseen that advances in military technology would one day make war impossible. He had also seen very clearly that a distinction had to be made in the capitalist world between "the intractable militarists and potential partners in peaceful coexistence."

With this argument, the Soviet-Chinese dispute on the criteria to be applied in the matter of peaceful coexistence had reached its climax. The Chinese had raised the affair to the ideological level, thus making it a matter of fundamental importance. Exactly as had been the case in the matter of the People's Communes, what was now at issue was the leadership of the international Communist movement, except that this time the problem directly concerned an aspect of live current policy, which, moreover, had already been implemented. Much more prestige depended on the cancellation or continuation of this policy than had been at stake in the question of the People's Communes. Khrushchev had to act.

When the Paris Summit Conference collapsed shortly afterward, in the spring of 1960, some Western observes saw in the fiasco the first effect of the Sino-Soviet dispute. Khrushchev's rampageous behavior was in such striking contrast to the coexistence line the Kremlin had previously been propagating. There was, in fact, no contradiction between efforts to achieve peaceful coexistence and the foreign-policy tactic of trying to attain one's ends "by peaceful and bloodless means," i.e., by political pressure. Also, the kind of statements made by leading American statesmen in the weeks before the summit conference probably dashed Khrushchev's hopes of Western concessions in the most important areas of current international policy. The summit diplomacy—which had so much promise for him—threatened to miscarry completely. Should he fail in Paris, his position in the Communist camp in regard to the Sino-Soviet conflict would be considerably weakened—and that must be prevented at all costs. So Khrushchev took refuge in boorishness, torpedoed the summit conference, and, as a side effect, brought about increased pressure on the Western leaders. That he nevertheless had no intention of deviating from his declared policy of coexistence was shown by his manner during his subsequent visit to East Berlin.

The Chinese saw through Khrushchev's maneuver, and realized that he had by no means given up his hopes of direct talks with the United States, but had only postponed them. So they increased their attack. In June, 1960, they opened up with a barrage that far outdid the one they had fired off in April. At the General Assembly of the World Federation of Trade Unions, the Deputy Prime Minister Liu Chang-sheng reiterated the Chinese standpoint. It was, he said, time the Communist Parties finally crystallized their attitude to the fundamental question of war. It was wrong to load the question by asking whether Communists were in favor of wars or not. To aim at the total abolition of war while imperialism remained in existence was "a completely mistaken concept" that would lead to serious consequences, "such as we are already experiencing."

To begin with, Soviet reaction to the Chinese charges was confined to newspaper articles. Lenin's *Left Wing Communism, An Infantile Disorder* (of the Communist movement) was quoted. At the same time, the Kremlin was considering the idea of a conference of all Communist states, to which all the Party leaders would be invited to discuss the unity of the Eastern bloc. The purpose of such a meeting was clearly revealed in a *Pravda* leading article, which stated: "Among Socialist countries there cannot be two opinions on the question of war or peace." The Soviets seemed determined to close the ranks of the Communist parties and to win support for their own views on the foreign-policy theory and practice of Communism.

A conference of Eastern-bloc countries did take place in June, 1960, on the occasion of the Rumanian Party Congress in Bucharest. All the leaders of the pro-Soviet, Eastern-bloc countries showed up. Peking only sent a member of their Chinese Politbureau, Peng Chen, and, for the first time, Albania made it plain to the world that she sympathized with the Chinese point of view: the Albanian Party was represented not by Enver Hoxha but by Hysni Kapo.

The Chinese delegates seemed to be following a definite line at this conference. They realized from the beginning that they would be in an isolated position at a conference consisting almost entirely of East European parties loyal to Moscow. What they wanted was a bigger conference which would also be attended by Communist parties whose interests would make them prefer the orthodox, militant line being followed by Peking. Peking's tactical short-term aim was the calling of such a conference; and this aim was realized with the decision to summon all Communist parties to a meeting in Moscow in November.

The decision that Khrushchev had hoped to achieve in Bucharest had now been put off. During the Bucharest conference, the Soviet leader probably came to realize the full extent and gravity of the dispute with Peking, to judge by the steps the Soviets took in the weeks that followed. A large number of Soviet specialists working in China were recalled, on the pretext that the Chinese were trying to influence them ideologically against the Kremlin. A number of Chinese students left Soviet universities. The periodical published by the Soviet-Chinese Friendship Society ceased to appear. Without giving any reason, Chinese scientists canceled their plans to attend a congress of orientalists in Moscow. Soviet provincial newspapers openly declared that "even a country as large as China" could not build up socialism in isolation, without the help and support of the Soviet Union, at the very moment when the Chief Chinese planner, Li Fu-chun, was claiming in Peking that China could fulfill her economic plans with her own resources. Moscow sent out circular letters and, in some cases, despatched emissaries to try to swing over to the Moscow line those Party leaders whose attitude seemed to have become somewhat uncertain.

However, although there were signs that Moscow was trying to haul Peking back on to the right track—and was prepared to use pressure to do so—certain other measures were simultaneously set in motion to make it easier for the Chinese to reach agreement with the Kremlin. Moscow felt sure that these measures would not imperil the coexistence course. What they were intended to do was to remove any doubt that might exist as to Moscow's revolutionary fervor. The Soviets brusquely quit the Geneva Disarmament Conference just as the West was getting ready to table new proposals for a solution, proposals which the Soviets themselves had hitherto been insisting on and which, moreover, gave indication of Western willingness to compromise. In the Congo affair, too, the Soviets became more aggressive, while threatening to use intercontinental missiles if the United States dared to attack Cuba.

In the ideological sphere new formulations were announced, which would go some way to meeting Peking's orthodox interpretation of Marxist-Leninist foreign policy. The formula "peaceful coexistence is the highest form of the class struggle" was coined in order to show that the coexistence policy would lead not to a softening up of the revolutionary movement, but rather to a toughening of it. It was only wars at the international level that were to be avoided, not local revolutionary wars of liberation. Thus there was no inconsistency in pursuing both peaceful coexistence in the diplomatic sphere and the policy of unconditional, revolutionary solidarity in the Communist movement.

These ideological modifications were admittedly not without their dangers. The Kremlin's coexistence slogan had been considerably weakened, and must have seemed less convincing to the West. Then again, the Chinese probably saw these reformulations as a tactical move, designed in the first instance to restore Moscow's damaged ideological authority, in preparation for the impending summit conference of international Communism.

For their part, the Chinese were also maneuvering with the coming Moscow conference in mind. The campaign which had culminated in the statement that only cowards were afraid of the prospects of a world atomic war was stopped, first place now being taken by the questions of peaceful coexistence and the possibility of avoiding war. Yet the Chinese standpoint was still that coexistence could only be forced on the imperialists "temporarily" and "to a certain degree." This breathing space would in no way improve the prospects of the permanent, world-wide victory of Communism. These fundamental ideas of the Chinese Communists were given another thorough airing before the start of the Moscow meeting. The respective positions taken by Peking and Moscow explain why it was that when the Eighty-One Party conference did take place, it took weeks of hard wrestling to achieve a compromise. While the conference was still in session, *Pravda* and the Peking "People's Paper" carried on a vitriolic controversy which laid bare the central point of the dispute.

The outcome of the Moscow conference seemed at first to be that on the really important questions Moscow had won the day. Peaceful coexistence, in the form the Soviets had been propagating remained. The avoidability of wars remained, too, as well as the demand that efforts should be made to reach a relaxation of tension, disarmament, and a general agreement with the capitalist powers. But these successes had not been gained without concessions to the Chinese. Coexistence, the final communiqué said, was a form of class struggle; and while the idea of coexistence had hitherto been coupled with the idea of "competition," the word now was "conflict." Also, for the first time in a very long time there was mention of "world revolution." Whereas Khrushchev, following his visits to Western Europe and the United States, had previously said of several Western statesmen that they had come to hold "realistic views," the Moscow communiqué contained not a word on that topic. The stress was now put on the aggressive and militaristic nature of imperialism, which had not changed in the slightest. The "aggressive, imperialistic circles" around the United States had become "the main bulwark of world reaction, the world's armed police, and the enemy of the peoples of the entire world." War could only be avoided by means of a determined resistance to the aggressive powers of imperialism, and that resistance must be more strongly put up than ever before. Moscow went even further to meet Peking's wishes. Some kinds of military action and, as Khrushchev defined it a few weeks later, "the just war of liberation," were accorded priority over the bloodless parliamentary road as a means of seizing power.

What was hammered out in November, 1960, as the general line for world Communism had a most militant appearance. But even without the Soviet-Chinese controversy, the Communists' world revolutionary program would have still been more militant than the one announced at the previous comparable meeting in November, 1957. Current problems were no longer the same. In 1957, following the setbacks in Poland and Hungary and their effects on the other Eastern-bloc countries, the important aim had been to find a common platform for the Communist parties in power, before Communists everywhere could devote themselves to the world revolutionary aims of classical Communist ideology. Only this can explain why the Chinese so energetically defended Khrushchev against his opponents in 1957. However, following the consolidation of the positions of the Communists in the individual satellite states, and especially since the elimination of the "anti-Party groups" in the summer of 1957, and the consequent strengthening of Khrushchev's position, the urgent matter was no longer how the Communists' position could be made secure and how the internal relations between Communist parties should be organized. The question now was how the hostile, outside world should be dealt with, and how Communism could be fostered outside the borders of the Communist states. The Moscow Declaration of November, 1960, laid down a common terminology. The fact that the tone of this terminology was much sharper than that of the 1957 declaration was at least partly due to the economic, strategic, and political improvement in the Kremlin's international position, and the Soviets' consequent feeling of superiority.

This may also give a clue to the real cause of the Sino-Soviet dispute. The realization of the growing strength and power of the Eastern bloc gave both powers new confidence and fresh impetus. Each of them believed they had made considerable progress toward obtaining their common goal. But on the question of the means to be used and the speed at which the goal should be reached—that is where opinions parted. Peking believed that the superior political and military power of the East should be used to confront the West more defiantly and ruthlessly. The Chinese Communists were in favor of "brinkmanship," believing that the West's consciousness of its relative weakness would not let it risk any countermeasures that might unleash an atomic war. Their own revolutionary experience and China's internal instability led the Chinese to feel that they must ruthlessly exploit the West's inferiority. They felt that the East's advantage might no longer exist if they waited. Mao therefore has thought that the dangers of the long road by way of peaceful coexistence are greater than those involved in the direct road, even if he himself should be overtaken by a world nuclear catastrophe.

Moscow seems to think the danger of nuclear war too great to risk. The Soviets are well aware of the West's military strength and take account of it in their political actions. The short route by way of "violent revolution" seems to them much more dangerous than the long way round. The success of their efforts to build up an empire over the past forty years has strengthened their confidence that they can reach their goal just as surely through the coexistence struggle as by the road of bloodshed and revolution.

The Soviets tried to bridge the gap between their views and those of the Chinese on the central problem of Communist strategy and tactics. Although they continued to insist on peaceful coexistence as the general line for Communists everywhere, they deferred to the Chinese by putting greater stress on revolutionary solidarity than they had originally envisaged. The attempt to combine the two views created a dilemma. Nobody recognized this dilemma more clearly than the chief Yugoslav ideologist, Kardelj, who published his views in a pamphlet called *War and Socialism*. Kardelj stated that however much one tried to please both sides by attempting to amalgamate the concepts of coexistence and revolution, one missed the essential point of the conflict between China and Russia until a solution could be found to the real problem: how far revolutionary solidarity embodies the risk of global wars, and why; and whether coexistence or revolution must be given priority at the decisive moment. The Kremlin reacted with unusual violence to Kardelj's analysis. It is significant that the November, 1960, declaration did not contain as much as a word on this problem. It was obvious that the rift in the Eastern bloc could only be whitewashed over, not properly repaired.

Revolution or Coexistence

The controversy between the Chinese and Soviet parties also had its effects in the underdeveloped countries. In Asia, Africa, and Latin America, political and social structures of the past were being rebuilt. New states were being born, nationalistic movements were gaining ground, and the demand for self-determination and independence could no longer be resisted. The birth of these young nations offered a very promising field for Communist infiltration; and it is not surprising that the Eastern-bloc countries took immediate advantage of the opportunity.

Moscow and Peking both realized that what was happening in the underdeveloped countries was the start of a historical process. Both watched with great satisfaction as the struggle for freedom being waged against alien masters was intensified. Both saw the opportunities that agrarian revolutions in these areas would offer Communism, although they also realized that certain elements were likely to stand in the way of socialist development and prevent Communist elements from gaining access to governmental power. The Soviets and the Chinese followed the same line of reasoning, based on classic Marxist-Leninist theory, regarding the transition of a colonial territory to an "independent" Communist state.

Divergencies between them in other areas notwithstanding, Moscow and Peking are still of one mind in regard to the basic aims of Communist strategy in the underdeveloped countries. When it comes to the question of how these aims are to be realized, there is a very plain difference of opinion between them. The dispute about the possibilities and effects of peaceful coexistence was therefore accompanied by another, this time on the tactics to be employed in the underdeveloped countries.

The classic theoreticians of Bolshevism had worked out a formula in which, first, a bourgeois-democratic revolution must overthrow the old regime, and after its successful conclusion, the way to a socialist revolution can be open. This theory is faithfully followed, both in thought and in propaganda, to this day, and it was in accordance with it that the "revolutions" in the East European countries took place after World War II. Mao Tse-tung, on the other hand, had early developed a new strategic formula for the Chinese area, which, while it did not completely diverge from the classic theory, postulated another way of reaching power. In 1940, Mao developed a theory which called for the inclusion of the so-called "national bourgeoisie" in the revolutionary struggle, until the Communists actually seized power, and even beyond. Loyal capitalists might even be allowed to take part in the government for a certain period, in order to strengthen the "anti-imperialist and anti-feudal front." The Chinese made this new tactic, the so-called "Four Class Campaign," the guiding principle of their theories on the way the Communists should act in the colonial and semicolonial territories.

Moscow was not entirely happy about this specific claim of the Chinese, but made it clear that in principle the Soviets would support Mao's tactical line. During the Korean War, the Soviets actually used Mao's ideas, and even developed them further. They reformulated the previous slogan of "unity from below" under the leadership of the Communists, who would now defend the interests not only of the workers and peasants but also those of the "capitalists." Neither ideological beliefs nor class origin was henceforward to be the criterion of revolutionary zeal, but only the will to join up with an "anti-imperialist movement." This new concept gave rise to certain difficulties when it appeared tactically more favorable to develop a "united front from above" (that is, an alliance or collaboration with nationalist organizations or individuals in the government of an underdeveloped country not under the guidance or control of the Communists), than a "united front from below." There was a danger that the Communists would find the road to power barred against them. A dispute broke out between the Soviets and the Chinese on this aspect of Communist policy in the underdeveloped countries. There was no disagreement that a temporary alliance with the class enemy should be entered into for the purpose of attaining power in a country: that had long been agreed in principle. What the two sides did *not* agree about was the conditions under which this alliance should be accepted, the precise time when it should start, and—even more important—when it should end. Exactly as in the main controversy on coexistence itself, the tricky point here was where coexistence should stop and revolution begin in the underdeveloped countries.

The Kremlin's thesis was that in these countries time was on the side of the Communists. The competition between East and West, especially in the economic sphere, would be decided in favor of the Communists. Since this was so, it was wrong to take any risks. Admittedly, Moscow never denied that in certain conditions a government might have to be overthrown by force or by a war of liberation; but there was no longer much enthusiasm for the idea, even if it was still valid in theory, and was still being suggested for the revolutionary movements in the underdeveloped countries. Moscow was also quite optimistic about the eventual effect of collaborating with the national bourgeoisie in cases where this group had taken control of a country without Communist direction. In *Bases of Marxism-Leninism,* published in Moscow in 1959, there was even a statement that a "peaceful transition" offered "greater advantages" than violent revolution, in that it allowed "a radical reshaping of society with the least sacrifice by the workers."

The Chinese Communists were not as optimistic as the Soviets. For them, wars of liberation were the means by which revolutionary victory would be won. They felt it their duty to take this road, even if it increased the danger of localized wars. But more than anything else, it was the collaboration with the national bourgeoisie, the "revolution from above," that the Chinese were unable to swallow quite as easily as the Soviets. It may be that their own experiences in the Kuomintang period was the deciding factor here. The Chinese were afraid that under the bourgeois leaders, the situation of the liberated peoples might become stabilized, the revolutionary impetus might die away, and there might arise a desire for collaboration with the West. If that happened, it would block the road to power for the Communists—or at least make the revolutionary struggle more difficult. "The revolutionary spirit is the soul of Marxism-Leninism," the Peking ideologists warned: it was a dangerous business to allow the flame of revolution to die down.

In a pamphlet, *The Victory of Communism in China*, published in 1959, Liu Shao-chi, the most important Chinese leader after Mao Tse-tung, demanded the speediest possible transition from the bourgeois-democratic revolution to the socialist revolution. Too long a pause, he said, must never be allowed. The prime condition for this quick transition, he maintained, was that the Communists already assume the leadership during the period of democratic-bourgeois revolution. To this, *Pravda* replied in August, 1960, that "at the beginning of every nationalist movement," control should be in the hands not of the Communists but of the bourgeoisie. In the countries liberated from colonialism, the struggle would not "for a very long time" be concerned with the bourgeoisie or with capitalism, but with the remains of the medieval feudal system still existing in these countries. The Communists must therefore be prepared to accept a long period of collaboration between the proletariat and the progressive elements of the national bourgeoisie.

There was a definite clash of opinion here, but what was really at issue was a difference of stress in the tactics of seizing power. Moscow never completely excluded the possibility of violent revolution, and Peking never denied the possibility of a bloodless transition. Where Peking differed from Moscow was in believing that this possibility would only occur under certain special conditions. The ideological concept of the Chinese only envisaged two such cases: first, when the political leaders in a country were "contained by revolutionary forces," and, second, when a capitalist country was already "encircled by socialism." It was this thinking that explained why the Chinese accepted a relatively mild method of dealing with their neighbor countries, but demanded an orthodox militant approach to the countries not "encircled by socialism." These differences of outlook on the possibilities of the Communist seizure of power are not only manifested in the theoretical disputations carried on between Moscow and Peking journals, but also in the way the two centers evaluate current political situations.

When the Middle East crisis broke out in the summer of 1958, these differences became public for the first time. A good example of their effect was given by what followed the events in Iraq in 1959. In the spring of that year, the Iraqi Communists had been given a considerable boost by a revolt in the Mosul oil fields area. This revolt had been initiated by nationalist forces as a protest against Prime Minister Kassem. After the crushing of the revolt, the Communists demanded that they should be given seats in the government, and that the ban on political parties should be lifted. Kassem refused. Following hints contained in the Eastern-bloc press, especially in Polish papers, serious differences arose among the Iraqi Communist leaders. The "left" wing thought the time had come for the Party to adopt more energetic measures vis-a-vis Kassem, and to start a "socialist revolution." At the beginning of 1959, the Iraqi Communist Party published a resolution which indicated that this "left-wing group had managed to influence the top men of the Party. Peking newspapers made great play with this militant declaration by the Iraqis, and gave plentiful evidence of Chinese agreement with it. Moscow ignored the declaration as such, and increased Soviet propaganda efforts to ensure the full support of the socialist countries for Kassem's Government in its struggle against imperialism. In the middle of July, a bloody rising, unquestionably instigated by the Communists, broke out in Kirkuk. The army quickly crushed the rising, and the Communists suffered a heavy defeat. Kassem disarmed the Communist-controlled militia and ordered it to be dissolved. At the end of July, the Iraqi Communists published a new resolution which contained both severe self-criticism and the admission that there had been serious errors in the tactical conception of the revolutionary fight. This time it was the Soviet press which hastened to publish the Iraqi resolution, and the Chinese who said not a word about it. The Chinese public never got to know about the Iraqi comrades' access of self-accusation.

At this period, it is unlikely that the Chinese had any direct influence on the Iraqi Communist leaders. The Iraqi decision was taken by the Iraqi leaders on their own initiative. Subsequently, the Soviets exploited the setback suffered by the Iraqis to give added weight to Moscow's views on the world-revolutionary struggle. The example of the Iraqis was repeatedly referred to in the debate on the strategy and tactics to be used by the Communists in the underdeveloped countries. There were warnings against the premature use of slogans supporting a "socialist revolution," and Peking was admonished to realize that the defeat suffered by the Iraqi Communists must be taken as a lesson for several parties in the East and in Latin America.

Shortly after the happenings in Iraq, another event showed that the Sino-Soviet dispute was still in full swing. In October, 1959, the Kremlin altered its policy on France. Khrushchev told the Supreme Soviet that he supported de Gaulle's Algerian plan. The French Communists performed a clever about-face and acknowledged that they had heretofore assessed this question incorrectly, just as the Kremlin had. When the Soviets welcomed de Gaulle's offer to the FLN to open negotiations on self-determination, the reason seemed clear. They wanted to create a favorable atmosphere for Khrushchev's forthcoming visit to France, since a Franco-Soviet *rapprochement* would contribute to the undermining of Western unity. To the Kremlin, this seemed to be more desirable than support for the Algerian liberation movement. Peking stuck to the position it had held prior to October, 1959. Shortly after Khrushchev's change of heart, the Chinese made known their view that de Gaulle's Algerian proposals were nothing but "a trick from A to Z." Anyone, they said, who did not unconditionally extend sympathy and help to peoples engaged in a heroic struggle with imperialism was lacking in a sincere desire to maintain and strengthen peace. When Khrushchev, on his return from France, once more paid his tribute to de Gaulle's Algerian policy, the Chinese reaction was to point out that if revolutions by colonized peoples did not receive unreserved support from the Communists, the world revolution would never be carried to a triumphant conclusion.

Peking's bitter disappointment at Khrushchev's "conciliatory" attitude in the Algerian question was augmented by Chinese anger at his behavior during his journey through the Asiatic continent at the beginning of 1960. The Soviet leader had ostentatiously advanced into an area which the Chinese regarded as their sphere of influence. Not only that, but he followed coexistence policies in India and Indonesia, two neutral countries with which China was at that time in open conflict. Khrushchev did not give the slightest evidence of sharing the interests of his mighty ally in New Delhi or Djakarta. On the contrary, he took every opportunity to advertise the efforts of the Soviet Union to bring about peaceful coexistence between all nations. Khrushchev's appearance in Asia directly impinged on Chinese interests, and the already strained relations between the two parties undoubtedly worsened as a result.

Tirana Supports Peking

As the relations between Moscow and Peking grew more tense, the more self-assured the Albanian leaders became. They had given the first sign of their denial of Moscow's claim to a monopoly of Communist wisdom on the occasion of the Rumanian Party Congress in Bucharest, in the summer of 1960. At the meeting of international Communists in November, their opposition came out into the open, and was reiterated at the Albanian Party Conference in February, 1961. The Kremlin, forced to take countermeasures to try to bring the defiant satellite to its senses, instituted boycott and reprisals.

It was Peking's attitude toward Moscow that shaped the attitude of Tirana. Enver Hoxha used the conflict between the two rival powers to take sides with the one whose views seemed to correspond more closely with his own interests, although his sympathy with Peking was not entirely tactical. There were some emotional points of contact that went beyond the merely tactical. The rise of the Albanian Communists and the way they had seized power resembled the victory of the Chinese comrades in many points, both having fought for the victory with their own resources—in Mao's case, even against Moscow's advice. Hoxha had not demanded assistance from the Red Army either to reach or to maintain his position, but without the vigorous help and advice of the Yugoslav Party, the Albanians would never have amounted to anything and Hoxha would not have won. However, the help the Yugoslav partisans provided was mainly confined to ideological and organizational advice on how to seize power. It was left to the Albanians themselves to put this advice into effect. This they managed to do, with the result that Albanian self-confidence grew, and, as so often happens, their one success led the Albanian Communists to overestimate their power and their potentialities. They tended to underestimate the risks and pitfalls of an adventurous policy, in which respect they resembled the Chinese.

The remarkably strong national feeling so characteristic of both the Chinese and the Albanians is another factor which contributed to the growth of bonds of sympathy between the two.

More important than either tactical considerations or mutual sympathy in the creation of this unusual alliance, however, was another factor: the correspondence in their basic political and ideological beliefs. For the Chinese, the attitude of the Soviets in matters like the revolutionary procedure to be adopted in the underdeveloped countries or Western "imperialism" is a heretical "right-wing deviation" from the true teachings of Marxism-Leninism. To the Soviets, the views of the Chinese seem equally intolerable, and are considered hateful "Trotskyite left-wing deviationism." Their own interests lead the Albanians to side *a priori* with Peking's version of Communism.

It would, however, be a mistake to think that Tirana's agreement with Peking extends to all matters of detail. In the organization of agriculture, for example, the Albanians do not accept the People's Commune idea, believing that conditions which suit China do not obtain in their country. They feel that the Chinese assertion that the People's Communes could be used in other Asiatic countries in a similar condition of overpopulation may well be true, but they do not feel that this particular type of organization should be taken over *en bloc*, merely to please the Chinese comrades. In Albania, discussion of the problems of agriculture is carried on just as it is in the Soviet Union. Albanians whom I met occasionally boasted of carrying out the collectivization and mechanization of agriculture more flexibly than the other East European countries. In fact, my own observations convinced me that the socialization of agriculture is being more rationally carried out than in, say, East Germany.

The Albanians are only marginally interested in the problem of the correct methods to use in the underdeveloped countries or how to deal with the West. They only deal with this problem, even on a theoretical basis, when there appears to be some connection between it and the national and Party-political interests of the regime. Their method of reasoning always starts with what currently seems politically expedient, as in their attitude to Yugoslavia or Greece, and then proceeds by deduction to more general considerations—not the other way around, as in the dispute between the Soviet Union and China.

The insignificant place occupied by Albania in the tug-of-war between the Powers makes this cast of thought quite understandable. Even if they do not share Peking's views in all respects and ignore or only signify theoretical acceptance of some of them, it is still indisputable that the Albanian Communists fully accept the bases of Chinese thinking. They too believe the revolutionary spirit to be the foundation of Marxism-Leninism, for it not only appeals to the Albanian mentality, it also corresponds to the needs of the home and foreign policies of their leaders. The strict ideological and semi-Stalinist climate that prevails among the Chinese leaders and permeates the whole of the Chinese Party machinery seems to Hoxha to be just what is needed to cope with treacherous elements. The proximity of Tito's Yugoslavia, with all its revisionist ideas that could only too easily penetrate into Albania, almost automatically called into being a kind of negative polarity. This, however, only cohered into a definite framework and crystallized into a specific program when Peking became a center of "orthodoxy."

The sympathy of the Albanian Communists for the Chinese exegesis of Communism is accordingly understandable enough. But what has caused Peking to support tiny Albania so strongly ever since the Moscow summit meeting? To do this, China had to accept risks and the possibility of sacrifices. Albania is a long way off and in a sphere of influence claimed by the Soviet Union. Considering the state of economic difficulty that their own country has been in for years, the Chinese cannot have taken their decision lightly. Then, too, they knew that their new step would inevitably add fuel to the flames of their conflict with Moscow, since the help they were giving the Albanians unashamedly cut across the measures the Soviets were employing to lead the recalcitrant satellite back into the bosom of the mightiest Party. This particular aspect would make the dispute even more serious than before, in that it would damage Soviet interests and Soviet standing in the field of practical politics far more directly than any amount of theoretical disputation. These difficulties and the great significance of a fresh controversy between Moscow and Peking were well understood by the Chinese. Nevertheless, the Chinese did not flinch. They went on, perfectly aware of what they were doing and by all appearances having calculated the risk involved.

What were the motives behind this? To appreciate them, one must remember that the controversy between Moscow and Peking was basically concerned with the correct interpretation of the common teaching. It is in the nature of Communism that only one universal opinion on a subject is admitted to be valid at any one time. This being so, the stubborn fight the Chinese put up to defend their position on the interpretation of Marxism-Leninism not only embodied a challenge to the Kremlin, but also amounted to questioning the Soviets' claim to be the leaders of world Communism.

Ideology and power are very closely correlated. The power-political monopoly position of a Communist central organization is only safe when the ideological center is also in a position to exercise control over the Communist parties, through the medium of personalities acceptable to the center. One example of this was the case of Rakosi. It will be recalled that after the Twentieth Soviet Party Congress had decided on a new strategical and tactical general line, the Kremlin came to the conclusion that Rakosi, the leader of the Hungarian Party, was no longer fit to hold his position because his mentality, his abilities, and his political methods might undermine the uniformity of the new general line of the entire Eastern bloc. As we know, it was Janos Kadar who was selected by the Kremlin as a suitable upholder of the new line; and this occurred long before the Hungarian uprising.

This intimate association of ideology, power, and control played an important part in the conflict between Moscow and Peking. The Chinese were not only concerned with their own ideological concepts, but were also out to gain adherents among the leading personalities of the individual Communist parties, the intention being that these adherents would enable the Chinese center to get control of their parties. It was only this—and not the question of some "deviationist" theory—that would furnish a basis for seriously challenging Moscow's leadership of world Communism.

An illustration of the way the Chinese went about trying to gain adherents is given by the split in the Indian Communist Party in the course of the Sino-Soviet dispute. Within the Indian Party there arose a "pro-Chinese" wing led by Ranadive, who concentrated his efforts on influencing certain parts of the subcontinent. Ranadive was in close contact with Peking, and he received his instructions from there. This "left-wing" group wanted to prepare the way for Communism in India by revolutionary activity, such as strikes and violent agitation against Nehru. They had no time for "coexistence with Nehru." Another group, the pro-Soviet section, was led by Ghosh, for many years the Secretary-General of the Indian Communist Party, and was supported by the majority of the Party. There was also a neutral group led by Nambudiripad. The extent of the split in the Indian Party at the height of the Russo-Chinese conflict is indicated by the fact that the hitherto undisputed leader of the Party, Ghosh, was actually removed from his post (even if only for a short period) and replaced by the "neutral" Nambudiripad, who would vote neither for Moscow nor for Peking.

There were similar, though less obvious, happenings in the Indonesian Party. The Secretary-General, Aidit, supported the Soviet line and had the majority of the Party with him. Other members of the Politbureau, such as Sudisman and Njoto, made no secret of their liking for the militant policies of the Chinese. Similar tendencies were evident in Cuba, the Communist bridgehead in Latin America. Blas Roca, the experienced leader of the Cuban Communists, stuck to the traditional pro-Soviet course. At the

Cuban Party Congress in 1960, however, it emerged that other prominent Party leaders, such as Anibal Escalante, were in sympathy with the ideas of the Chinese.

The Chinese made particular efforts to influence the revolutionary movement in Africa, where they paid more attention than the Soviets to the task of winning over the ultraradical African leaders. Africa was also the scene of a particularly noteworthy difference of opinion between the Soviets and the Chinese. At the Conference of the Afro-Asian Solidarity Council in Conakry in April, 1960, the two rivals could not agree on the formulation of the final resolution. The Chinese representative rejected the Soviet draft out of hand. This draft had said, *inter alia*, that after the ending of the Cold War, the economic development of the Afro-Asian countries must be pushed ahead with all speed. This, said the Chinese representative, might lead the peoples of Africa and Asia to the erroneous conclusion that the imperialists really believed in disarmament, peace, and economic competition. According to an Indian observer, the attitude of the Chinese greatly astonished all the delegates "and not least the Soviet delegates."

There were other auguries that could not help but cause the Soviets more disquiet than the squabbles in one or two neutral parties: symptoms that appeared within the very perimeter of Soviet power, namely, within those East European Communist parties that still preferred Stalinist methods. Apart from the Albanians, these were the Czech and East German parties, both of which gave indications of siding with the Chinese. At the end of 1959, upon sending Mao birthday greetings, Walter Ulbricht, the leader of the East German Communists, had emphasized the "enrichment of Marxism-Leninism and of socialist unity" that had come about through Mao's theories. Those who could interpret shades of meaning in the formulation of Communist statements must have been struck by the difference between this and Khrushchev's greetings. The Soviet leader wasted no words and spoke merely of Mao's "loyalty to Marxism-Leninism." On the tenth anniversary of the Chinese revolution, Ulbricht declared—no doubt to the chagrin of Moscow—that Khrushchev's trip to the United States had been undertaken "in complete conformity with Mao's understanding of Marxism." At the same time, East Berlin newspapers were full of praise for China's "great leap forward," which they considered an example for all the other Eastern-bloc states. Hermann Matern, a member of the East German Politbureau, went furthest when he declared in Peking that the concept of the Chinese People's Communes was exceedingly important and pointed the way to be followed by all Asian peoples.

The East German leaders, used to thinking in Stalinist terms, were no doubt gazing expectantly in the direction of Peking at this period. Their tendency to sympathize with Chinese ideas on current affairs was made evident in other cases too. For example, when the border dispute between India and China broke out, the East German Communists loudly supported the Chinese point of view for a number of weeks and only reverted to the more neutral and cautious Moscow line some time later.

At the November, 1960, summit meeting, the Soviet leaders had their work cut out to bring about agreement between the eighty-one parties. At the start of the conference, some Asian and Latin-American Communist parties were much nearer to the Chinese position than to the Soviet, and it took some hard tussling to get these minor parties to modify their orthodox positions, at least temporarily. But there was one Party against whom all argument failed: The Albanian leaders refused to give way. Hoxha stuck by Mao. Peking succeeded in creating a breach in the phalanx that Moscow had so painstakingly built up on the basis of Soviet principles, Soviet ideas, and the opportunities for Soviet control. From now on, nobody could charge the Chinese with supporting a "left-wing orientation" of Marxism-Leninism out of purely nationalistic motives, for there was now a group. Tiny as the group might have been, it was all the more important to the Chinese for not having grown out of some patent circumstance, such as geographical proximity.

The rise of "left-leaning concepts" in the Eastern bloc forced Moscow to take sterner measures. The Albanian example, they felt, must not be allowed to spread. In the spring and summer of 1961, the Soviets did all they could to tame the rebellious Albanians; but their efforts were in vain. So it was that the Twenty-Second Party Congress saw some really violent attacks on Albania.

V

Albania and the Twenty-Second
Party Congress

BEFORE IT BEGAN, the Twenty-Second Party Congress did not look
as though it would produce any surprises. The main item on the
agenda, approval of the new Party program, had already been discussed and rediscussed in the weeks before the Congress, and, in
any event, the new program had been approved and ratified by
the Central Committee of the Soviet Party at a special meeting
shortly before the Congress opened.

During the Congress, however, things worked out quite differently than planned. "Discussion" of the main item had obviously
been struck out in order to deal with other matters, much more
important in the minds of the leaders. One surprise followed another. Khrushchev and the other Party leaders started an attack on
so-called "dogmatism" and on the supporters of out-of-date orthodox ideas and terrorist methods in Communist policies. It was not
optimistic prognostications about the future of Communism that
animated the delegates' speeches: the mood in the hall was determined by the still unpaid accounts from the era of Stalin.

The Soviet leaders' attacks were directed against two exponents
of reactionary Bolshevism: the so-called Party enemies—Molotov,
Kaganovitch, and Malenkov—who had been expelled in 1957;
and the Albanian Communists, who still fostered Stalinism and
its negative manifestations.

Nobody had foreseen that events would take such a turn at
the Congress. The Western experts tried to puzzle out what it all
meant. Had the pundits been wrong when they maintained that
Khrushchev's position was as secure as ever? Was it possible that
his former opponents still had enough influence in the Party to be
a threat to Khrushchev, in spite of their having been banished to
insignificant positions in the provinces? Or did the attack on the

Albanian Party mean that the militant Chinese were exerting pressure that was forcing Khrushchev to mobilize all his forces to prevent resistance to his policies within his own area of influence?

These questions ceased, however, as the background of this Congress—perhaps the most important of the Party Congresses of the Soviet Communist Party—gradually emerged from the speeches of the functionaries. It became evident that the course of the Congress was not going according to plan, and that something was happening during the Congress to steer it in a direction that the organizers probably had not intended when it began.

The Attacks on Albania

On the eve of the Twenty-Second Party Congress, Communist delegations from all over the world were received in Moscow with fraternal cordiality and great pomp and ceremony. Albania was the only country that had no delegation. The Soviet Communist Party had not sent an invitation to their Albanian comrades, and the proceedings on the very first day made it plain why. In his initial report to the Congress, Khrushchev attacked the Albanian leaders and accused them of deviating in a number of important matters from the universally accepted line of the entire Communist movement. They had acted contrary to the decisions taken at the Twentieth Party Congress, condemning the consequences of the "hateful cult of personality." They had continued to employ the Stalinist methods that the Soviet leaders had been trying to eradicate for so long.

Surprising as these public charges against Albania were, it appeared as though Khrushchev regarded them as a last effort to persuade Albania to renounce her erroneous ways. His accusations were still couched in general terms, and he was not yet speaking in bitterness or anger. If anything, he appeared to be animated by anxiety and sorrow. What the Albanians were required to do, it seemed, was to "give up their mistaken ideas" and return to the paths of "the unity of friendship with the Communist Party of the Soviet Union."

The conclusion that suggests itself is that Khrushchev's comparatively restrained attack on the Albanians was in fact directed at Peking. The sobering experiences the Kremlin had had in the previous eighteen months, during which neither persuasive words nor pressure had been able to induce the Albanians to change their ways, must have made it obvious to Khrushchev that this new attack would not do it either. The only thing that might have enabled the Soviet leaders to achieve their aim would have been the benevolent mediation of the Chinese.

Two days after Khrushchev's opening speech, the chief Chinese delegate Chou En-lai rose to convey the Chinese comrades' greetings to the Congress. It only needed a few sentences by the prominent Chinese politician to make it clear to the audience that the Chinese Party was by no means willing to accept Soviet views on certain important matters, nor to take on the role of mediator in the Soviet dispute with Albania. In his speech, Khrushchev had spoken of his hope for a "normalization" of relations with the United States. Chou En-lai castigated the American Government as the "most despicable enemy of peace," and called the policies of President Kennedy "more aggressive and foolhardy" than those of his predecessor. Whereas Khrushchev had been of the opinion that it was possible to normalize East-West relations, Chou En-lai maintained that "every measure taken by the American imperialists shows that we are still faced with the danger of war and that the peoples of all countries must be increasingly on their guard." While Khrushchev had only made a passing critical reference to Yugoslav revisionism, Chou En-lai bracketed both "the Yugoslav revisionist clique" and American imperialism together as the main enemies of socialism.

Chou En-lai spoke even more plainly when he openly condemned the way the Soviets had dealt with the Albanian Communists. The unity of the socialist camp, he said, embraced "twelve fraternal countries, from the People's Republic of Korea to the German Democratic Republic, and from the People's Republic of Vietnam to the People's Republic of Albania." This unity must be fostered like a tender plant. There must under no circumstances be disputes or any other actions which might damage it. "We think," he went on, "that if a quarrel or difference of opinion should arise between brother-parties or brother-countries, this should be settled by consultation, patiently and in the spirit of proletarian internationalism, on the basis of equality and unanimity." Public, one-sided criticism of a brother-Party would neither serve the cause of unity nor help to solve problems. Making public the fact of a quarrel between brother-parties of brother-countries in plain sight of the enemy could not, he maintained, be regarded as a serious Marxist-Leninist attitude. It could only dismay those near and dear to them and hearten the enemy. "The Communist Party of China sincerely hopes that the brother-parties which are separated by differences or quarrels will once more come together in the spirit of Marxism-Leninism and on the basis of mutual respect, independence, and equality. That, in my opinion, is the attitude we Communists should adopt in this matter."

Two days later, Chou En-lai again gave evidence of his displeasure at the whole tenor of the Moscow Congress, in general, and Khrushchev's methods, in particular, when he visited the Lenin-Stalin mausoleum in Red Square and laid two wreaths. One commemorated the father of the Russian revolution, Lenin; the other was in memory of Joseph Stalin. The ribbon on this wreath bore the inscription "To the great Marxist-Leninist, Joseph Stalin." On October 23, 1961, hardly a week after the opening of the Moscow Congress, the chief Chinese delegate left Moscow and returned to Peking. The Soviet press gave as the reason for this sensational development the impending session of the Chinese National People's Congress, a meeting that never took place. The Chinese themselves gave no reason for Chou En-lai's departure, but the reception he was accorded on his arrival in Peking provided ample explanation of it. Mao Tse-tung showed up at the Peking airfield in person, accompanied by every one of the top men of the Chinese Party, an open demonstration that the Chinese Communists wholeheartedly applauded Chou En-lai's attitude in Moscow.

This calculated affront by the Chinese Communists did not go unanswered. The Soviet leaders did not actually go straight into a direct attack on Peking; the Kremlin's anger was vented on Tirana instead. A flood of wild accusation and vituperation poured over Albania. One Soviet speaker after another gave voice to the Soviet spleen over the Albanian leaders. Hoxha and Mehmet Shehu were apostrophized as "hypocrites," "schismatics," "traitors," and "slanderers of Marxist-Leninist ideas." The Soviet Party leaders' expression of their bitter feelings over the hostile and stubborn attitude of the Albanian Communists increased in violence. Tirana, it was said, was refusing to give up its Stalinist methods. Mikoyan devoted his remarks to the Albanians' deviations from the "Leninist course" of the Communist movement, and especially their refusal to obey the "norms of Communist life." What Mehmet Shehu understood by the "norms of Communist life," Mikoyan added, could be seen from what he had said at the Fourth Albanian Party Congress, "If anyone is not in agreement with our leaders in any point, we shall spit in his face, bash him on the jaw, and if necessary we shall put a bullet through his head." Kuusinen claimed that Albanian citizens had been arrested for advocating friendship with the Soviet Union.

Khrushchev reserved his most vicious attacks for his final speech at the Congress. He accused Hoxha and his clan of "malicious, dirty attacks" on Communism, "such as not even our enemies, open or concealed" carried on. He described the Tirana leaders as nothing less than Judases, whose slanders were preparing the way for them to be able to "claim alms from the imperialists." Khrushchev summarized the reasons for his attacks on Albania in the statement that the Albanian leaders did not like the decisive condemnation of "the cult of Stalin and its pernicious consequences." Hoxha and Shehu, he alleged, supported "despotism and misuse of power": in fact, it had now reached the point where they could only maintain their positions by using force and despotic methods. Anybody who fell afoul of the Albanian leaders was cruelly persecuted. Those Albanian Communists who had created the Party, the ones who had fought against the German and Italian fascist invaders, had almost without exception fallen victim to the "bloody crimes" of Mehmet Shehu and Enver Hoxha.

He gave a particularly shocking example of the Albanian leaders' use of Stalinist methods. Some years previously, the Central Committee of the Soviet Party had appealed to the Albanians on behalf of Lira Gega, the former member of the Albanian Politbureau, who had been condemned to death along with her husband. This woman, Khrushchev declared, had for several years belonged to the leading organizations within the Albanian Party and had played an active part in the Albanian people's fight for liberation. The Soviet leaders had been animated by the humane belief that the shooting of a pregnant woman was not in consonance with "the principles of the Communist idea." "Even in the period of blackest reaction, the Czarist minions never dared to torture revolutionaries or to execute pregnant women. But in this case, in a socialist country, a woman who was to be a mother was condemned to death and executed."

Khrushchev's speech left no doubt in the minds of his audience that he regarded a reconciliation with the present Albanian leaders as quite out of the question. If the Albanian Party leaders were to abandon their Stalinist methods, that would be tantamount to giving up their control of state and Party. He was convinced, he said, that the time would come "when the Albanian Communists and the Albanian people will have their say. When that time comes, the Albanian leaders are going to have to answer for the harm they have caused to their country and their people in the cause of the building up of socialism in Albania."

This seemed to mean that Khrushchev had abandoned all hope of reaching agreement with Albania. Moreover, he seemed convinced that the Chinese Communists had stiffened the Albanians in their refusal to take the extended hand of reconciliation. At least this was the sense of the words Khrushchev used, as the only speaker at the Moscow conference to direct his remarks at the Chinese Communists in connection with the "Albanian question." In his speech the leader of the Chinese delegation, he said, had expressed his sorrow that the matter of relations between the Albanians and the Soviets had been publicly discussed during the conference. If he understood it correctly, what the Chinese comrades were afraid of was that the present state of relations between the Albanian Party and the Soviet Union might prejudice the solidarity of the socialist camp. "We share the anxiety of our Chinese friends and can appreciate their care for the strengthening of our unity," the Soviet leader went on. "If our Chinese comrades wish to play a part in the normalization of relations between the Albanian Workers' Party and its brother-parties, nobody is in a better position to contribute to the solution of this problem than the Chinese Communist Party itself. That would serve the interests of the Albanian Party and would be in line with the interests of the comity of Socialist countries."

Enemies of the Party

The course taken by the Twenty-Second Party Congress made it clear that the violent attacks on Albania, and the warning to China that went along with them, had not initially been foreseen as part of the proceedings. But there was another surprise, equally unexpected. Parallel to the increasing severity of the attacks on Tirana was a series of condemnations of Stalin and his political followers, in which speakers vied with each other in revilement and abuse.

At the start of the Congress, Khrushchev had done no more than glance at the problem of Stalin and "the consequences of the Stalin cult." He reminded his audience that Lenin had recommended to the Central Committee of the Bolshevist Party to remove Stalin from the post of Secretary General, and he condemned the "errors and distortions" that Stalin had permitted to creep into the work of the Party. Khrushchev even found a few words of praise for Stalin. "Of course Stalin did a number of good things for the Party and the Communist movement; we must do him that much justice." At this point, there was no sign that the Twenty-Second Congress would give rise to "a second bout of destalinization," as did the Twentieth Party Congress in 1956.

This new turn did not take place until several days later. It is fairly certain that what sparked it off was Chou En-lai's laying a wreath on Stalin's glass coffin. The movements of the Soviet machine that now followed were like the moves of the pieces on a chess board. It was the same step-by-step tactic that had brought on the decision on "destalinization" at the Twentieth Congress. A mass of detail on the bloodiest epoch in the history of the great purges between 1936–38 was once more brought to life. The attacks on Stalin culminated in Khrushchev's proposal that a monument should be erected in Moscow "to the memory of those comrades who were sacrificed to terror and despotism." There was an almost simultaneous suggestion that Stalin's body should be removed from the mausoleum in Red Square.

One of the most interesting developments was the method by which the condemnation of Stalin was linked with accusations against so-called enemies of the Party. Zaburov and Pervukhin were ignored by almost all those who spoke. They had already confessed their errors and had been appropriately dealt with. For the first time, Voroshilov was named as a "conspirator." Shortly after he had been elected into the Presidium of the Party Congress, he was forced to sit in silence while the verdict on him was pronounced. In his final speech, however, Khrushchev showed compassion with Voroshilov, pointing out that he had admitted his errors and suggesting that the Congress should accept the regrets he had expressed. He had done much for the Party and for the Soviet people, and he, Khrushchev, believed that in future Voroshilov would "stand up for the cause of the Party."

The real, crushing weight of the attack was directed at the other three members of the so-called anti-Party group, Malenkov, Kaganovitch, and Molotov. Malenkov was described as the close collaborator of the head of the GPU, Yeshov, at the time of the great purges. Later, the Congress was told, he also worked very closely with Beria, and had been particularly involved in the decimation of the White Russian and Armenian Party in 1937. He had also played a part in other bloody purges and was responsible, together with Beria, for the purges in Leningrad in 1949 and 1952. Kaganovitch was described as a sadist who had been responsible for countless mass arrests, and was accused of having initiated the terrible purge in the Russian Federal Soviet Republic and the Ukraine.

But the severest criticism was reserved for Vyacheslav Molotov, for many years the Soviet Foreign Minister and the only surviving colleague of Lenin. He it was who was most closely identified with Stalin's crimes, although the main weight of the attack on him stemmed from the fact that he was regarded as the ideological leader of the anti-Party group. It was obviously intended to link the crimes committed in the Stalin era with a definite type of ideological thinking, and Molotov was to be shown to be the main exponent of that thinking.

Mikoyan opened the ideological attack, defining Molotov's failing as underestimating "the strength of Socialism" and consequently overestimating "the forces of imperialism," an erroneous premise which led him to equally erroneous conclusions. This was particularly true of his judgment of international developments, his opinion of the possibility of attaining peaceful coexistence and preventing world war, and his attitude to the various forms that could be taken by the transition to socialism. Molotov, he said, completely rejected peaceful coexistence, thus agreeing with the views of foreign opponents of peaceful coexistence, who regarded it as a variation of the Cold War and as a condition of "armed peace." Pospelov, the Party ideologist, charged that Molotov was convinced that global victory of Communism could only be won by means of wars.

In the final speech on this point, Khrushchev summarized the most heinous parts of Molotov's views in two points. First, Molotov had tried to justify what had been done during the Stalin era and had also maintained that similar things were possible in the future—a view which Khrushchev described as "foolhardy and criminal." Second, Khrushchev once again declared that the principle of coexistence between states having different social systems was an absolute necessity from the foreign policy point of view. Under present-day conditions, peaceful coexistence was of vital importance, something that the "hopeless dogmatists" could not grasp. They clung to generalities about imperialism and persisted in "turning their backs on life." This was exactly the point of view taken by the stubborn Molotov.

The Last Stand Against Stalinism?

At first sight, it may appear that the conjuring up of the unsettled account of the past and its conjunction with the heavy attack on the "anti-Party group" was nothing more than manifestation of the continuing struggle for power inside the Kremlin or the releasing of long-pent-up personal dislikes. But the history of Russian Bolshevism contains many illustrations of the way personal antagonisms can be traced back to political and ideological causes. They were always at the root of serious dissensions within the structure of totalitarian power, and the Twenty-Second Party Congress served to confirm this fact. The sensational developments at the Congress should not be allowed to obscure the real purpose of the meeting, namely to discuss and ratify the new Party Program, which would lay down the general line for the coming decades. Even though the matter of the Party Program was completely pushed into the background in the course of the Congress, we must be quite clear that it was the very fundamental differences of political and ideological views on the new program that were the real cause of the turbulent scenes at the Party Congress. They were the starting point of both the campaign against Stalinism and the anti-Party group and the attacks on the leaders of the Albanian Party and their protectors in Peking.

One of the most significant points of the new program was the abandonment of the regime of terrorism and despotism, and the intention to build up a system of Party absolutism supported only by Party authority based on organized compulsion and total ideologization. This meant a return to the concept that Lenin and his professional revolutionaries had envisaged, and which had been accepted by all Communist parties as the model for a Communist social system. Stalin had shifted the accent in this party-political basic concept. The Party and its sociopolitical task were pushed into the background and the secret police held the power. Terror was made absolute. Whereas Lenin and his companions had thought of brute force as the ultimate stage in organized compulsion, Stalin made it the ruling element in political and social affairs.

It is fairly clear from the speeches made at the Twenty-Second Party Congress that many of the Party members and functionaries were skeptical about the theses contained in the new program foreshadowing the road to total Communism, and that this skepticism was principally concerned with the program's ideological content. It contained a number of points that could not help but evoke uncomprehending head-shaking among Marxist-Leninists trained in orthodox ways of thought.

Khrushchev hinted at this reaction when he said in his speech that certain individuals misunderstood the theses in the program, which envisaged the realization of internal Party democracy when the proletarian dictatorship had been replaced by "self-administration in the People's State" linked to the Party. But it is quite understandable that convinced Communists should have been deeply shaken, for this new concept struck at the roots of "proletarian dictatorship." The "scientifically based" prophecies on the course of human history now seemed to be robbed of their certainty. To many a functionary it must have seemed that what Khrushchev was doing was to undermine the very foundations of the edifice constructed by Marx and Lenin.

The doubts and anxieties thus harbored by many functionaries should not be taken to imply resistance or even opposition within the Party ranks, for any misgivings they had were directed against a group of men who sat very firmly in the saddle. Khrushchev carried through a thorough-going clean-up of the Party machine at all levels in the months before the Twenty-Second Party Congress, and the ease and lack of concern with which he did this confirmed that on this occasion his primary concern was not to maintain the dominant position of the Party leaders, but to create an obviously secure basis for his plan to employ the Party's power in a new direction. This intention was made even more evident by the new program and Party statutes. It turned out that there was a direct connection between the personnel changes and the items set down for discussion at the Party Congress, for only the "versatile organizer" (as he is now called in all statements on the future cadre policy) is capable of ensuring the implementation of the new Party Program.

What Khrushchev seemed to be telling his functionaries was that while the new program admittedly contained ideas and theses that were novel and even radical, these new ideas must be given every assistance in getting themselves established, because this was the only way Communism could achieve final victory, not only in the Soviet Union but also in the rest of the world. Anyone who did not wholeheartedly cooperate in this was not only clinging to the outdated, but was consciously or unconsciously threatening to relapse into outmoded Communist strategy and tactics. This was the reason why the specter of the past was conjured up at the Congress and why all present were deliberately reminded of the terrible details. The campaign against the "enemies of the people" proved to be both an appeal and a warning to all functionaries.

The "enemies of the people" were dealt with a long time back.

Their condemnation was at bottom only a shadow play *pour encourager les autres*. But there is every possibility that centers might come into existence outside the Soviet Union around which skepticism, including that in the Soviet Union, might crystallize. Those Communist leaders who claim to possess the "untainted teaching" are already beginning to lay claim to the title of Lenin's genuine successors. For two years, every functionary in the Soviet Union has known that Peking is making this claim. This is the second and much more important reason for the campaign against the "enemies of the Party."

One of the charges made against Albania at the Twenty-Second Party Congress was that she was the only one of the countries in the socialist camp that had not published the full text of the Draft Program of the Soviet Communist Party. Khrushchev indignantly pointed out that only disconnected extracts had appeared in the Albanian press, which had "deliberately given a distorted impression" of the work and aims of the Soviet Communists.

What Khrushchev did not reveal was that the Chinese had done the same thing as the Albanians. The Peking "People's Paper" had certainly printed the entire text of the Soviet Program but it had not added any commentary on it—a sin of omission which, considering the importance of the document for world Communism, was of profound political significance. Moreover, Peking made it known in various ways how much it mistrusted the new Soviet Program. A month before the publication of the Draft Program in the Soviet Union, the Chinese, who had obviously seen it in advance, loudly declared that while the Program might be all right for the Soviet Union, the Chinese People's Republic could not accept it as binding on them at all.

This assessment of the Program is very different from the one contained in the Soviet Party's claim that the Program, as Khrushchev put it, represents "a new stage in the revolutionary theory of Marx, Engels, and Lenin." The Soviet leader proclaimed, not without *arrière-pensée*, "To anyone who wants to know what Communism is, we can proudly say 'read our Party Program.'"

The views for which Molotov was condemned by the Soviet Party leaders were in the main the same as those which had brought the Chinese into opposition to Moscow. The attacks on

Molotov and Albania were in all probability intended for Peking, since Moscow regarded the "anti-Program front" composed of Molotov, Albania, and Peking as a point around which deviationist ideas and teaching might potentially crystallize. This fear was very evident in the speeches by Kuusinen and Ilyitchov at the Congress.

The sequence of Moscow's counterattack began, logically enough, with the initial condemnation of Molotov, who was the one most heavily incriminated. That was the line of least resistance. Then came the attack on Albania, the most isolated and backward satellite. Albania was of no great political importance anyway, and her loss would not cause the Soviets much pain. The tactic of the two-pronged attack seemed to be sufficient for the Soviet Union's purpose of making clear to her only politically and ideologically significant rival her determination not to let herself be turned aside from the course she had taken. It was her most forceful demonstration so far and was intended to make it very plain to the Chinese that the Soviet Union's new domestic and foreign policies must be raised to the level of policy to be followed by the whole of international Communism.

Tirana Strikes Back

In view of the fact that relations with Moscow were steadily getting worse, the Albanian Party leaders had no reason to expect that the Twenty-Second Party Congress would lead to any easing of the strained relations between Tirana and Moscow. When Enver Hoxha and his chief colleagues, unlike the other Communist Party leaders, did not receive an invitation to the Congress, he must have realized that trouble was brewing. At a reception in the Chinese Embassy in Tirana on October 1, he made a speech in which he warned that anyone who raised his fist against Albania would be smashed.

Nevertheless, even Hoxha was probably surprised at the actual severity of the Soviet attack. He and the other Party leaders reacted to the Kremlin's charges immediately, keeping in strict step with events at the Congress. Hoxha responded to Khrushchev's comparatively mild reproaches at the start of the proceedings by sending a telegram of greeting containing assurances of friendship with the Soviet Party. "No power on earth, no calumnies or intrigues" could separate the Albanian Party and people from the CPSU and the Soviet people. The telegram not only made no mention of Khrushchev's accusations, it did not so much as refer to Khrushchev by name. This was an unmistakable hint as to whom the Albanian leaders regarded as the calumniator and intriguer.

The delegates at the Congress were told of the arrival of the telegram by Suslov, who added that it contained a "mixture of hypocrisy and slanderous innuendoes." The next day, the Albanian leaders made their countermove, which took the form of a resolution by the Central Committee in which Khrushchev's attacks were described as "anti-Marxist slanders," which could only serve the purpose of enemies of socialism, imperialists of every complexion, and the Yugoslav revisionists. The Central Committee announced that in view of the serious situation that had come about as a result of the Soviet attacks, it could no longer remain silent, and would now ruthlessly "present the truth about relations between the Albanian Workers' Party and the leaders of the Soviet Party to the entire Communist movement and the public of the world, and brand the anti-Marxist and anti-Albanian machinations of Khrushchev and his clique." The Albanians were prepared for a "long and difficult fight," the resolution concluded, but "neither defamatory attacks nor blackmail nor threats by Nikita Khrushchev and his supporters" would make them weaken.

The Albanian Communists also played a trump card that Chou En-lai had already put down on the table. The Chinese representative had clothed his reproach in polite terms, but the Albanians were not so considerate. By revealing to "the enemy" the fact of differences of opinion between the Soviet and Albanian Communists, they claimed, Khrushchev had "brutally broken the terms of the Moscow Declaration of 1960." Since Khrushchev had not kept to his side of the agreement, he had declared "open war" against the unity of the international Communist movement. However, the very tone of the resolution made it plain that the Albanians were not very confident that their trump card would take the trick. Moscow easily countered this by saying that they had honestly tried to settle the differences, but each time they tried, the pig-headed Albanians had thwarted them almost before they started.

The reaction of the Albanian leaders may have given the appearance of self-assurance and resolution, but in fact Moscow's charges could not leave Hoxha indifferent. He was well aware that in so far as they referred to the terror and despotism reigning in Albania, the charges were justified and, moreover, that they would be re-echoed within the country. For this reason, he was forced to keep a firm grip on Albania's internal situation and to justify his unrelenting attitude toward Moscow. Accordingly, there took place mass meetings and demonstrations in order to hammer into the Albanian peasants and workers "unequivocal loyalty to the policy of the heroic Workers' Party and to the Marxist-Leninist standpoint of its Central Committee." Speeches, radio talks, and newspaper articles unceasingly called on the people "to fight to the bitter end to defend Marxism-Leninism."

At the same time, the Tirana leaders were not so incautious as to use ideological slogans to whip up the people. They used a method that had already proved its worth in the long struggle against Yugoslav revisionism. Their propaganda urgently warned the people of dangers to the country's national existence. This was not confined to assurances that the beloved Fatherland would be defended to the last drop of blood. All reservists up to the age of thirty-five were called up for military service. Not that the military value of this step should be overrated. Against which enemy from without was it directed? Against the Soviet Union? What did the puny Albanian forces think they could achieve? Western calculations put the Albanian Army at four divisions of 10,000 men each, plus some 20,000 border police and security units. Calling up the reservists would not add much to the fighting power of these forces. What is more likely is that the measure was really taken as a precaution against the possibility of trouble within the country itself. But the final reason is probably to be found in the desire to give the people a psychological jolt by means of a hysterical campaign of "vigilance." Nothing is more certain to arouse the emotions of the Albanian people than the suggestion that the country's national existence is in danger.

On November 7, on the eve of the twentieth anniversary of the founding of the Albanian CP, with all these preparations made, Hoxha thought it was time to launch a detailed answer to the Moscow charges. In a cleverly laid out and dialectically brilliant speech lasting four hours, Hoxha gave his version of the reasons for accusing the Kremlin of "sinister plans, demagogy, hypocrisy, and slander." In all the essential matters under dispute Hoxha steadfastly maintained his position as a militant, radical theoretician.

The removal of Stalin's body from its tomb in Red Square he described as an "inhuman game." "For us," he said, "Stalin was and will remain, both as a practical politician and theoretician, one of the most outstanding leaders and one of the most outstanding personalities not only in the Soviet Union but also in the whole Communist and labor movement, one of the most ardent defenders and the greatest theoretician of Marxism-Leninism."

Hoxha rejected the peaceful coexistence concept because it was "fraudulent and anti-Marxist," and because it would "end in the negation of the class struggle." Khrushchev's definition of the different forms of the transition to socialism by peaceful means would arouse in the workers "the illusion that they can attain power by taking the road of the parliamentary majority." The Albanian workers, however, had never harbored any illusions as to the nature of imperialism, any more than they had ever been afraid of it. The same could not be said of Khrushchev, as was illustrated by the example of Germany and Berlin. Who was it who had shied away from the responsibility for finding a solution to the German problem? "Do you think it was we, who have always wanted the quickest possible solution? Or was it our accusers, who are always retreating from the problem and putting off grappling with it from year to year?"

Hoxha criticized the Kremlin's attempts to realize "internal Party democracy" and reminded his listeners of the machinations by Polianski during the decisive days of the summer of 1957, while the struggle for power was going on in Moscow—matters which had hitherto been unknown in the West. Hoxha was thus giving a hint that he would not hesitate to reveal further compromising details if necessary. But matters had not yet gone that far, as Hoxha himself plainly stated. "We are not without friends in the

Socialist camp. They have not left us in the lurch, and they will not leave us in the lurch in the future." These words left no doubt about who had encouraged the Albanian leaders to adopt such a bold attitude.

In one form or another, the campaign went on for months, with new quotations and new charges, although these never strayed from the basic theses contained in Hoxha's November speech. The Kremlin also refused to back down and continued to repeat the accusations. And still the real opponent was not directly addressed. There were only occasional hints by Moscow that although Albania must serve as the whipping boy, the real object of the Soviet campaign was located in Peking. It was not until February, 1962, that Moscow stopped pretending that Albania was completely alone, defending a hopeless position. The Kremlin's chief ideologist, Suslov, declared in a speech at a meeting of sociologists in Moscow, "the great majority of brother-parties condemn the Albanian leaders" and criticize "those who sympathize or agree with the anti-Leninist standpoint of the Albanian leaders." Almost at the same moment *Izvestia* announced that the Albanian Communists were by no means unique in their ideas and were "only parroting the ideas of others." It was not hard to guess who the "others" were.

The Reaction of the Chinese Communists

To judge by appearances, the Chinese had also not foreseen the surprising course taken by the Twenty-Second Party Congress. A reasonably reliable indication of this was the composition of the Chinese delegation. Chou En-lai, the leader of the delegation, regarded as one of the most intelligent and agile-minded of the men around Mao, was probably more open to a compromise with Moscow than Liu Shao-chi, who headed the Chinese delegation to the Moscow summit meeting in November, 1960. Chou En-lai was also accompanied by the First Secretary of the Kwangtung Province Party, Tao Chu, who had repeatedly shown conciliatory tendencies toward Moscow. On the other hand, the delegation also included Peng Chen, who, as Peking's representative at the

Bucharest meeting, had remained unshaken in the face of violent attacks. Kang Sheng had also attracted attention with a speech at the Warsaw Pact Council meeting in the spring of 1960. Thus, although Peking appeared to have provided for all eventualities, their choice of Chou En-lai to lead the delegation indicated that they were not expecting any "fighting talk" during the Moscow Congress. This situation changed when Khrushchev opened his attack on the Albanians and remained unmoved by Chou En-lai's reproaches. Peking drew the necessary conclusions and Chou ostentatiously left Moscow, leaving the field to his "hard" colleagues Peng Chen and Kang.

The change of Chinese attitude was made plain not only at the Congress but also in official Chinese propaganda. It was a week after the conflict between Tirana and Moscow came out into the open before the official Party newspaper, *Jen Min Jih Pao,* published its comments on the "Albanian question." The paper carried the part of Khrushchev's report that contained the criticism of relations between Moscow and Tirana. On the same page, the paper printed the malicious telegram of greeting and the Albanian Central Committee's caustic declaration to the Moscow Congress. The rest of the page was devoted to extracts from speeches made at the Congress dealing solely with Albania. This proceeding was clearly the first result of the discussions held within the highest Chinese committees after Chou En-lai's return from Moscow.

During the remainder of the Moscow Congress and in the weeks that followed, Peking was still trying to give the appearance of wanting to be the honest broker and mediator in the dispute. Moscow's accusation and the no less violent countercharges by Tirana were published side by side, even if the Chinese left no doubt about where their sympathies lay. They lost no opportunity of stressing the "unshakable friendship" between the Albanian and Chinese parties. Albanian delegations that happened to be visiting China at this time were received with rapturous enthusiasm. Prominent speakers in Peking declared that the Chinese people would always be "trustworthy comrades-in-arms of the Albanian people." The Peking "People's Paper" announced with satisfaction that of the seventy-nine brother-parties which had delivered addresses of greeting or sent congratulatory telegrams to the Moscow Congress, thirty-one had not mentioned relations between the Soviet Union and Albania.

At the end of November, 1961, Peking openly took up its position at the side of the Albanian Communists. On the seventeenth anniversary of the liberation of Albania, the Chinese Central Committee sent Hoxha and the leaders of the Albanian Party a telegram signed by the three leading men in China, Mao Tse-tung, Liu Shao-chi, and Chou En-lai. The telegram stated that the Albanian Party was a "glorious member of the great socialist community," and that in their "southwestern outpost of the socialist camp," they had "made important contributions to the defense of the security of that camp." The Albanian Party, the telegram went on, remained "true to Marxism-Leninism and to the principles of proletarian internationalism." This was the reason why "the people of China and Albania are closely linked brothers in the great socialist Community." With an obvious sideways glance at Moscow, the telegram ended with the words, "May the fraternal friendship between the Chinese and Albanian peoples endure forever."

Peking's patronage was not confined to the political and ideological field. Albania's more pressing need was for effective economic and financial assistance, and Peking was prepared to supply it. A representative economic delegation from Albania set off for Peking and successfully negotiated an increase in the Chinese comrades' aid measures. The extent of this strengthening of the economic collaboration between the two countries was demonstrated to the world by the founding of a Chinese-Albanian shipping company. According to the agreement, the ships belonging to this company would be mainly engaged on traffic between China and Albania "in order to safeguard the enormous help that the Chinese brothers are giving Albania toward the fulfilment of the third Five-Year Plan and to break the imperialistic and revisionistic blockade."

China's increasing efforts to help her tiny European ally were paralleled by her increasingly truculent attitude toward Moscow. The Chinese were evidently out to make clear the ideological motives that were conditioning their stand. Matters came to a real head at a conference of the World Peace Council in Stockholm in December, 1960. The point at issue between the Soviets and the Chinese was the form in which Communist world revolutionary activity should be continued. The leader of the Chinese delegation, Liao Cheng-chi, thought the "peace movement" should increase its efforts to appeal to the broad masses of the people and not rely on "leading personalities of the higher social strata." Only the masses could effectively combat imperialism. For similar reasons the Chinese delegate criticized Soviet summit diplomacy and Khrushchev's efforts to bring about an American-Soviet *rapprochement*. "The belief that a couple of great powers can settle international problems without regard for the opinions of the smaller states is erroneous and cannot be realized," he said. The days when a few great powers controlled the fate of the world are long past.

Another Chinese Party functionary, Liu Ning-ji, spoke in opposition to Soviet disarmament policy. "Certain people" thought that the "national independence movement" must take second place to efforts to achieve total disarmament. "That is a wrong and dangerous assumption." In the fight against imperialism, all the oppressed nations must strengthen their armed forces, for a "powerful national liberation movement can bring imperialism to its knees much faster than all your talk about disarmament." The American policy of intimidation must never be allowed to cow anyone or to keep him from carrying out a revolution and supporting it with all available resources.

At about the same time as the controversy between Moscow and Peking was being exacerbated on this particular point, the Chinese leaders thought it an opportune moment to reiterate their views on the three central points of Sino-Soviet disagreement, and to do it with considerable publicity. The results demonstrated that the gulf between their views had not grown any smaller. The Chinese Party center still used the traditional method of disguising their argument under a cloak, their accusations against Moscow being actually contained in charges ostensibly directed at the United States. The basis for this polemic analysis was provided by the interview President Kennedy granted to Khrushchev's son-in-law and by the speech in which Adlai Stevenson opposed Red China's entry into the United Nations. But in fact, the form and content of the Chinese remarks showed that they were primarily intended for the rivals of the Chinese leaders in the Kremlin.

It was in this context that the Chinese for the first time undisguisedly raised their views on strategy and tactics to the level of a principle of international Communism.

This, then, was the position at the turn of the year 1961–62. Practically speaking, the Chinese had reopened the dispute between Moscow and Peking at the point at which it had first become fully public in April, 1960. In November, 1960, there had been a hard fight to iron out the differences and get nearer to each other's point of view, so that the rift in the Eastern bloc could be pasted over. Now the paste had peeled off again and the rift was once more visible. Indeed, the differences between the two had obviously been made even greater and more irreconcilable by the proceedings at the Twenty-Second Party Congress, and the attack on the Albanian leaders.

Will the East Split?

Albania has gotten herself into a precarious position and the question is whether the leaders will be able to hold their course, and if so, for how long. Not only did the Soviet leaders put their smallest ally into a most serious political position at the Twenty-Second Party Congress, but their furious attacks brought on further consequences that went much further than the reprisal measures already ordered before the Moscow Party Congress. The Soviets recalled their diplomatic representatives and made the Albanians withdraw theirs. Albania was expelled from COMECON and from the meetings of the Warsaw Pact states, which meant that the Albanian Communists had been politically outlawed.

It is sometimes said that the Kremlin's measures against Albania have gone further than Stalin's against Yugoslavia in 1948. This is only partly true. Moscow never broke off diplomatic relations with Belgrade, even when Soviet-Yugoslav relations were at their lowest ebb. It must be remembered that the Eastern bloc, at this time organizationally united in the Cominform, had formally expelled Yugoslavia from the community of socialist countries by a unanimous vote. Belgrade was declared an ideological and political defector, and the maintaining of diplomatic relations made no difference to that fact. In the case of Albania, the situation is reversed. Even though there is no longer any political line of communication between Moscow and Tirana, the Albanian Communists have not been driven into the wilderness.

The difference between the 1962 situation and that of 1948 is quite clear. In 1948, Stalin's will was the will of the Eastern bloc. "Common decisions" was merely a euphemism for orders given from one central authority. The situation is different today. Moscow is obliged to tread more cautiously in its handling of a rebellion in one of its satellites. The era of the lone decision that nobody dared to oppose is past and gone. There is no longer an unquestioned chain of command in the community of Eastern-bloc states. Fronts have been formed. Opinions vary, and are only brought into some sort of consonance after tough bargaining. The reaction to Khrushchev's moves in the Albanian dispute has shown that in some cases not even that is possible any more. Whereas Belgrade stood completely alone in 1948, Albania, small and politically insignificant though she is, has an ally among the confederation of Communist states, and one whose words carry considerable weight. At the Twenty-Second Party Congress and afterward, Peking left not the slightest doubt that the Chinese do not accept Albania's expulsion from the Communist community, and, what is more, that they mean to stand by their protégé with every means they possess.

Khrushchev understands this, which is the reason why he confined his countermeasures to breaking off diplomatic relations or to action in regard to organizations such as COMECON and the Warsaw Pact, to which China only belongs as an observer without voting rights. The sentence on Albania, however hard the consequences may be for the Albanians, was still not an irrevocable and final verdict. It was much more than a slap on the wrist, of course, but nevertheless the blow did not have behind it the shattering force that unanimous damnation by all Albania's political friends would have given it.

This means that the Albanian leaders still have a chance. Tirana need not feel itself absolutely lost. Albania still has allies—friends whose views cannot be ignored in the Eastern bloc. Even more important at the moment, perhaps, is the willingness of these allies, even though their own economies are in distress, to spare some of their scanty resources for their comrades-in-arms on outpost duty at the other end of the world. As long as this willingness remains, the alliance between the great rival in Peking and the tiny Mediterranean country will represent a serious obstacle to Soviet policies.

The difficulties that lie ahead for the "orthodox fraction" must not be underestimated. As far as one can judge, the help the Chinese can give Albania will never be able to compare with the support the Soviets used to provide. They lack the resources, and, above all, they lack the unlimited means of surely and swiftly transporting the necessary commodities to Albania. The economic boycott put on by the European Eastern-bloc countries is also bound to give rise to serious problems. Moscow has stopped air transport from and to Tirana. How then will the Chinese specialists and technicians get to Albania, in view of the fact that no Western airline company is willing to set up a regular air service to Tirana? And above all, how will the promised goods and equipment be carried from China to Albania? Those who know Chinese marine capacity are agreed that the newly founded Albanian-Chinese shipping company, which will have to be built up entirely out of Chinese resources, is not likely to be able to cope with the task.

Under these circumstances, it is not surprising that after the break with Moscow, Tirana began to put out feelers to see if it might be possible to arrange matters with Greece, Italy, or even with other countries in the West. Albania, the Tirana Foreign Ministry announced, was willing to take up diplomatic contact with any state that showed "good will" toward her. These are preliminary steps paving the way to a field in which the hard-pressed Albanians are very interested. If it were possible to expand trade and economic relations with the Western world, they feel, then it might be possible to get through this period safely and, at the same time, lighten the burden on their allies in Peking.

There are already some signs that the Albanians may pull it off.

They have concluded an agreement with Italy to increase trade by 50 per cent. Greece is interested in Albanian oil; and in other West European countries, including West Germany, there has been an awakening of interest in Albania in commercial and industrial circles.

Still, these attempts at making contact must not be allowed to obscure the fact that the Tirana regime will only be able to feel sure of its continued existence as long as it stays loyal to its Chinese protector. Hoxha and his functionaries can feel safe as long as Mao continues to support the Albanian revolt against Moscow. This political and ideological alliance is the factor which takes precedence over all other measures. Much as the methods being used by the Albanian Communist leaders may look like political brigandage, it is highly unlikely that in making efforts to improve relations with the West, Tirana is secretly preparing the ground in case the Chinese will one day no longer be able to help or Peking gives way to Moscow's demands. There is nothing in the way the Albanian Communists think and act to suggest this possibility, nor is there anything in the attitude of the Chinese that might give the Albanians cause to prepare themselves for disappointment. The Albanian Communists still think of themselves as the apostles of orthodox Peking teaching, to which, for better or for worse, they are bound. For them Albania is a kind of spiritual province of the Red Middle Kingdom, an important outpost and bridgehead in Europe, through which the "pure" teaching and correct Communist strategy and tactics can flow out into the Communist movement.

This undeclared motive behind the alliance between China and Albania explains why Moscow made such violent efforts to achieve a settlement of the Albanian question. Did only this moment seem to Khrushchev to be the right one to put the pressure on the Chinese partner? The Kremlin knew all about China's economic and domestic difficulties in the fall of 1961, after the harvest had failed three years running. The supply position in China was extremely serious. Western observers who returned from China at this time brought back deeply moving reports. In many provinces people were starving, not only in the country but also in the industrial areas, where working hours had to be shortened because the exhausted and emaciated workers could not keep up the pace, or because of lack of raw materials. In the heavily industrial area of Wu Han, the monthly rice ration was so drastically cut that it was only enough for three days. Sugar is only issued four times a year. The watery rice mush is thickened up with grass. China's available foreign currency reserves are being used to buy wheat from the granaries of the world, particularly from Canada and Australia. The regulations governing the import of food parcels have been greatly relaxed.

The Kremlin will undoubtedly have had similar reports on China's catastrophic supply situation. Now China will be more dependent on Soviet economic aid than ever, the Soviets may have thought, and the men around Mao will be more anxious than ever not to put any further strain on relations with Moscow. This made the attack on Peking's Albanian ally into a trial of strength. But if Khrushchev thought Mao would surrender, lose face, and award the prize to the Kremlin, then he was mistaken.

However, Khrushchev is good both at calculating the odds and at hedging. He will go a certain distance, but not all the way. It is a fair assumption, therefore, that even if Khrushchev may have cherished a faint hope that he might force the Chinese to retreat at this time, he risked starting up the campaign against Albania —coolly taking China's recalcitrant attitude into account and despite the danger that he might fail at the first attempt—in order to force the inevitable decision.

For the Kremlin, the Albanian Communists' rebellion against Moscow was more than an act of disobedience by a vassal who must be brought to heel. Albania became the visible symbol of a development within the whole Communist movement which must lead to the disintegration of the entire Eastern bloc, and to struggles that would set a new course in all the Parties. Nobody could foresee the outcome of this development more clearly than the Soviet Communists, experienced as they were in precisely this kind of thing.

This process of decomposition cannot even be arrested by the proclamation of the so-called "polycentric system." The highly intelligent leader of the Italian Communist Party, Palmiro Togliatti, had already put up this idea for discussion after the first destalinization in 1956, with a view to putting a brake on what seemed to him an inevitable development. In his view, more respect should be paid to the differences between Communist parties, and their individual views ought to be listened to with more understanding. But his cautious and vaguely formulated theses, brought out at the end of 1961, were coolly received in Moscow, where the Soviets had already had experience of an existing case of "applied polycentrism." The condition of Moscow's political and ideological relations with Belgrade had been a lesson to them. Yugoslavia's example had not only demonstrated that the Communist alliance would lose its impetus if the individual parties' demand for a separate headquarters were to be granted, it had also shown that the Communist idea and the Communist system cannot tolerate disintegration in any shape or form, since this must inevitably foster the dispersion of ideology and power.

The Soviet Communists could not incorrectly point out that the previous success of the revolutionary movement had been achieved on the basis of a universally accepted philosophy, the totalitarian structure of the Communist teaching, and uniformity of methods—all interpreted by one central point and absolutely binding on all. Finally, there is another consideration that plays a decisive part in Soviet thinking. Advancing disintegration and the consequent unavoidable hardening of fronts might well result in the gradual displacement of the claim to ideological and political monopoly by one central authority.

There are signs that Peking is thinking along the same lines, although this does not mean that the Chinese want to claim the monopoly position for themselves. The fact that they do not claim it is repeatedly evidenced by their terminology. Until quite recently, the Chinese were still maintaining that the Soviet Union must retain the "leading role" in the socialist camp. Nor should this be shrugged off as pure lip service. In Tirana, too, the Albanian leaders, in curious contrast to most of the other East European People's Democracies, still emphasize their acknowledgment of the Soviet Union as the leading power.

What is the explanation of this paradox? On the one hand, Peking and Tirana unmistakably reject the Moscow center's general line, while on the other, they admit the same center's "leading role in the socialist camp" just as they always did. Unless appearances deceive, the paradox is more apparent than real. Fully understanding the essential elements of Communist theory and practice, even the "orthodox fraction" maintains the principle that the Soviet Union, as the mightiest and most advanced Communist power, must stand at the head of the "Socialist camp." In spite of this, however, the "orthodox fraction" is convinced that the new general line of this leading power is wrong, because it involves too many risks and contains too many dangers. Stubbornly and with tactical and diplomatic finesse, the orthodox are offering resistance, the intention being to lead the mighty and fundamentally respected ally "back on to the right road."

I have the impression that in many Western analyses, this aspect of the three-cornered relationship between Moscow, Peking, and Tirana is not given sufficient weight. Quite understandably, the stress is generally laid on the differences between the two poles of the international Communist movement, simply because the West hopes that the controversy will produce political advantages which will benefit the cause of the free world. This is wishful thinking. However much the attitudes taken by the two sides may seem to be in direct opposition to each other, and however wide the rift between the rivals may yawn, the methods being propagated, no matter how dissimilar, are still aimed at achieving one common goal: principally, the destruction of the common enemy in the West. This common aim provides the strong tie between the centers, no matter how much they may outwardly seem to be at loggerheads: a circumstance that conditions their thinking every bit as much as their annoyance at having to carry on the controversy in the glare of publicity.

These two factors—the respect that is willingly paid to the Soviet Union as the leading power and the consciousness of being of one mind with regard to the goal to be attained—have also had their effect on the practical treatment of the conflict. Both centers of world Communism are reluctant to take the final step. Each of them is fully aware that a torrent of unforeseeable consequences would pour over both of them if it came to an open break. Accordingly, both sides probably find that the urge to find a solution in spite of everything plays a large part in all their thinking.

This tendency is fostered by the partial realization by both sides that their own position is not without its problems. Revolutionary Communism has reached the crossroads, but it is necessary to come to some decision. Moscow believes that in order to make any kind of convincing progress at all, it must take the road of a renewal and a strengthening of the competitive ability of the system. Khrushchev is certain that this is the only road to success and is pushing ahead his reforms with unquenchable vigor. The other side, from Molotov through Peking to Albania, only accepts the desirability of a reform of the theory and practice of Communism up to a certain point. They hesitate to take the same road, fearing obstacles which they may lack the strength to overcome. In particular, it seems to the "orthodox" impossible to keep in step with the leading power. Both sides have weighty arguments to support them. Their views collide with a resounding clash. In spite of the tone of the debate, which may sound to Western ears as though the differences are insoluble, each of the centers almost certainly recognizes the sincerity of the views held by the other.

We can, however, take it that one stage of the discussion, in which a certain amount of understanding was being displayed in the attempt to find an acceptable new general line, is now over. Time is not on the side of compromises. The development of the Sino-Soviet dispute has shown how difficult it was to work out a common platform even in the theoretical field. We may assume that the possibility of a compromise is still one of the subjects most thoroughly discussed both in Moscow and in Peking. There is too much at stake to allow things to take their own course. But what has already proved to be an unusually difficult task, even in the theoretical field, seems downright insoluble when the opposing views meet head-on in a burning question of political practice. This is what makes the Albanian question so very important for the Eastern bloc. Differences in political practice had already shown themselves to be constricting and dangerous. But the example of Albania proved for the first time a case that directly affected the leaders in all Communist centers. It is also a case that affects the foundations of a regime whose internal stability must be a precondition for effective and successful activity beyond its own borders.

There were signs, in the spring of 1962, that the Communist leaders were well aware of this. The Soviet ideologists have repeatedly laid out the reasons for the Soviet attitude on Albania. It was no accident that the most detailed statement of the Soviet point of view in *Problems of Peace and Socialism,* the theoretical paper of the international Communist movement, should have been written by its editor-in-chief, Rumyantsev. It had obviously become necessary to do something to try to allay the anxiety being felt in the ranks of the Communist parties abroad, who could perhaps understand the dispute but not the manner in which it was being carried on. Even Rumyantsev did not go into detail about the point that all functionaries must think is the most important: why the differences cannot be resolved "in comradely discussion." This is the weakest point in the whole of the Soviet argument. The fact that it was not mentioned leads one to conclude that not only abroad, but also in the Kremlin itself, many an ideologist and theoretician is tortured by the question whether it was really right to unleash the conflict with Tirana with such vehemence, or whether some other method would have been better. In Peking too, it is probable that they have been wondering whether the behavior of the Party leaders in the early stages of the Moscow-Tirana controversy, especially in the spring and summer of 1960, was really the most appropriate under the circumstances.

Such discussions, wherever they may be held in the councils of the Communists, are, of course, academic. Political developments have taken their course. Albania went from being a symptom to being a burden, and it was only the Soviets' open attack on the Albanians that led international Communism into a blind alley, from which neither of the authoritative doctrine holders seems able to retreat. This is the reason why both the rivals seem so reluctant to make a move. Neither of them dares to take the risk. It looks very much as if neither Moscow nor Peking knows how to put a stop to the dangerous process of disintegration. Each side is still trying to fortify its own position at conferences held in the separate centers, such as the March, 1962, meeting of the Central Committee of the CPSU and the session of the National People's Congress in Peking at the same time. What they are really trying to do, however, is to suppress their tormenting uncertainty about the outcome of the contest. The only thing that could produce a decision would be a new international council of the Communist parties. The fact that neither side seems in a hurry to bring this about is still another indication of their desperate anxiety about the possible consequences of such a gathering.

In the Eastern bloc, the storm signals are still flying. There can be no doubt that all concerned fully realize the consequences that might flow from a complete break, and yet, as things stand at the moment, a break seems more likely than a compromise. The mutual recriminations and accusations of having betrayed the grand idea and endangered the existence of the regime have now reached a stage where the thoughts and actions of the Communist leaders have taken two quite different directions. A continuing split between China and the U.S.S.R. over the Albanian question seems inevitable, as long as the basic Sino-Soviet conflict is unresolved.

INDEX

Abakumov, V., 99
Aidit, D. N., 137
Alarup mines, 40
Alia, Ramiz, 12, 14, 17, 58
Amery, Julian, 57
Argyrocastro, 71–72
Balli Kombetar party, 88–92
Balluku, Bequir, Lt.-Gen., 58
Bari, 57
Belishova, Liri, 13–14, 15, 59, 96, 102
Beria, L. P., 99, 147
Brioni, 69
Bulatovic, Peter, 101
Bulganin, N. A., 99
Bulgaria, 4, 73, 74, 75–77
Cerrik refinery, 38, 40
Cervanaka mines, 40
Chen Po-ta, 109, 110
Chiang Kai-shek, 107, 117
China, 10–11, 12–14, 17–18; Communes, 108–15, 120, 134–35; economic aid to Albania, 41, 43–49, 51; and Soviet dispute, 104–39; and Twenty-Second Party Congress, 142–69
Chou En-lai, 142–43, 146, 153, 156, 157, 158
COMECON, 39, 160, 161

Congo, 123
Couturier, Valliant, 80
Cuba, 123, 137–38
Czechoslovakia, 41, 48
Dedijer, Vladimir, 50, 80, 95, 107
de Gaulle, Charles, 132
Demi, Tahir, 15, 16
Dimitrov, Georgi, 84
Dishnica, Ymer, 90
Djilas, Milovan, 50
Durazzo, port of, 34, 35–37, 43–44, 48–49
East Germany, 19, 20, 41, 45–48, 73, 135, 138–39, 142
Eisenhower, Dwight, 22
Engels, F., 79, 151
Escalante, Anibal, 138
Fier plant, 41
Five Year Plans, 38–43
Fourth Albanian Party Congress, 21–23, 29, 40
France, 132
Fundo, Lazar, 80, 84, 93
Gagarin, Yuri, 10
Gega, Lira, 101, 144–45
Gerö, Eruö, 101
Ghosh, Ajoy, 137
Gjinishi, Mustafa, 90
Gomulka, Wladyslaw, 77, 78, 108

Greece, 4, 57, 70, 73, 74, 75, 77, 97, 135

Gretchko, Marshal, 18

Hoxha, Enver, 9, 10, 13–20, 21–22, 40, 54–55, 56, 58, 59, 60, 67, 69, 71–72, 104, 105, 122, 133, 135, 139, 143, 144, 152–56, 157, 163; biography, 79–103

Humphrey, Hubert, 110, 113

Hungary, 114

Ilyitchov, Leonid, 152

India, 133, 137

Indonesia, 133, 137

Iraq, 117, 131–32

Ismail, Kemal, 4

Italy, 6, 83, 87

Jakova, Tuk, Maj.-Gen., 98–99

Jello, Halim, Maj.-Gen., 15

Jugoff, Anton, 75–76

Kadar, Janos, 69, 136–37

Kaganovitch, L. M., 140, 147

Kang Sheng, 119, 157

Kapo, Hysni, Maj.-Gen., 9, 13, 17, 72, 122

Kardelj, Edvard, 80, 126–27

Kassem, Abdel Karim, 131

Kastriota, Georg. *See* Scanderbeg

Kellezi, Abdyl, 45, 97

Kelmendi, Ali, 82, 83, 84

Kemal (Ataturk) Mustafa, 55

Kennedy, John F., 22, 142, 159

Khrushchev, Nikita S., 10, 12, 16–19, 27, 34, 67, 68–70, 72–78, 99, 101, 110–18, 121–25, 132, 133, 138, 140, 141–59, 163, 167

Koniev, Marshal, 18

Korea, 142

Koritza, 71, 82, 83, 84, 85, 87

Kossovo, 5, 68, 89, 90

Kozlov, F. P., 117

Kupi, Abas, 88–89, 92

Kurbneshi mines, 40, 45–48

Kuusinen, Otto, 120, 144, 152

Lac plant, 41

Lebanon, 117

Legaliteti party, 88–92

Lenin, V. I., 11, 62, 79, 110, 119, 120, 122, 143, 147, 149, 150, 151

Leskovik, 71

Li Fu-chun, 123

Liao Cheng-chi, 159

Liu Chang-sheng, 121

Liu Chao-shi, 17, 130, 156, 158

Liu Neng-ji, 159

Liu Tan-tao, 109

Lleshi, Haji, 15

Macedonia, 68

Mehti Valley power plant, 40

Malenkov, G. M., 140, 147

Malinovski, Marshal Rodion, 18, 27

Mao Tse-tung, 10–12, 20, 108–16, 117–18, 126, 128, 130, 138, 139, 143, 156, 157, 164

Marko, Rita, 14

Martanash mines, 40

Marx, Karl, 79, 150, 151

Matern, Hermann, 139

Mehmet Ali, 4

Metohija, 68

Mikoyan, A. I., 110, 117, 144, 147–48

Miloti plant, 40
Molotov, V. M., 50, 80, 140, 147–48, 151–52, 167
Montenegro, 4, 5
Mugosa, Dusan, 85, 86–87, 94
Mukaj pact, 89–90, 97
Murad II, Sultan, 3
Mussolini, Benito, 7, 88
Nambudiripad, Sankaran, 137
Ndren, Dali, 101
Nehru, Jawaharlal, 137
Njoto, 137
Noli, Fan Stylian, Bishop, 5–7, 81, 82
North Epirus, 5, 70, 72
Nou, Bekir, 97
Novak, Roman, 22
Osmane, Adem, 15
Peng Chen, 17, 122, 156
Pervukhin, M. G., 147
Pishkashki mines, 40, 48
Plaku, Panayot, Maj.-Gen., 15, 67–68
Poland, 77, 107–8, 114
Polianski, Dmitri, 155
Popovich, Miladin, 85, 94
Pospelov, P. H., 22, 69, 147
Prenjas mine, 41
Rakosi, Matyas, 101, 136
Ranadive, Balachandra Trimbak, 137
Religious persecution, 54–56
Robespierre, 62
Roca, Blas, 137
Rumania, 73–74
Rumyantsev, Aleksey, 168
Sarand, 54

Sasseno island, 24–26
Scanderbeg, 3–4
Scutari, 54, 56, 57, 64, 65, 66, 82, 84, 85
Sejko, Teme, Rear Adm., 15
Serbia, 4
Shehu, Abedin, 97
Shehu, Mehmet, 15, 17, 19, 20, 21, 22, 41, 75, 76, 92, 100, 143, 144
Shikin, Joseph, 20
Shivkoff, Todor, 75, 76, 78
Shtylla, Behar, 15
Sigurimi (secret police), 53–54, 60
Sino-Soviet dispute, 104–39
Soviet Union, 10–11, 18–23, 62–63, 74, 77; aid to Albania, 50–51; and China, 104–39; naval bases in Albania, 23–28; reprisals against Albania, 32–43; Twenty-Second Party Congress, 140–69
Spahiu, Berri, Maj.-Gen., 98–99
Spiru, Nako, 96
Stalin, J. V. D., 10, 50, 54, 60–64, 66, 72, 79, 80, 101, 103, 105, 107, 111, 113, 118, 140, 143, 144, 146, 147, 149, 155, 161
Stevenson, Adlai, 159–60
Stoica, Chivu, 73, 74
Sudisman, 137
Suslov, M. A., 69, 153, 156
Tao Chu, 156
Tashko, Kochi, 14, 15, 59, 102
Teng Hsiao Ping, 17, 19
Tirana, 41, 54, 82, 84, 87

Tito, J., 17, 20, 50, 64, 67, 69, 80, 87, 89, 94, 95, 96, 97, 104, 105, 107, 135
Titov, G., 10
Togliatti, Palmiro, 164–65
Treaty of Tirana, 5
Tropoje mines, 40
Turkey, 73, 74, 77
Twenty-Second Party Congress, 140–69
Ulbricht, Walter, 19, 138
United States Sixth Fleet, 15, 23, 76
Valona, port, 5, 24–26, 28, 67, 87
Venizelos, Sophocles, 72, 73, 75, 78
Vietnam, 142

Vincani, Nedship, Gen., 97–98
Voroshilov, K. E., 147
Vukmanovic-Tempo, Svetozar, 89, 94
Wang En Mao, 110
Warsaw pact, 18, 23, 119, 160
Wied, Prince Wilhelm zu, 5
Wrangel, Baron, 5
Xoxe, Kochi, 69, 95–96, 98, 99–100
Yeshov, N. I., 147
Yugoslavia, 29–32, 135, 160–61, 165; aid to Albania, 49–50; revisionism, 64–70; wartime help, 86–101
Zog I, King. *See* Zogu, Ahmed
Zogu, Ahmed, 5–7, 81, 83